Adventures in Writing

By
JOYCE STULGIS-BLALOCK

ISBN 1-58037-387-9

Printing No. CD-404055

Mark Twain Media, Inc., Publishers
Distributed by Carson-Dellosa Publishing Company, Inc.

Table of Contents

Table of Contents (cont.)

Introduction to the Teacher

The Purpose of This Book:

This book was written to help teachers and children. It is a book of writing projects that can help eliminate most of the planning time for writing workshop or language arts time during the day. Projects include designing characters, settings, and plots for plays; inventing fairy tales, folktales, and ghost stories; creating science fiction stories and comic book heroes; and looking at characters from various points of view. While the students are working on the project, it enables the teacher to interact with the students and/or evaluate the work as it is being done on the spot. These are some reasons you may find this book very helpful:

1. **Each project is coordinated with a National Standard from the National Council of Teachers of English (NCTE), from which many state and national tests are developed.**

2. **The projects may take one or two weeks to complete. First and final drafts are required.**

3. **The book can be used over an entire year or even longer.**

4. **Students can work alone, with a partner, or in a small group to complete each project, but it is entirely up to the teacher as to how he or she plans to use the lesson.**

5. **The projects encourage a wide variety of creative options that really help motivate the students to complete the task.**

The Projects:

This book is a collection of writing projects that teachers may give their students during the school year. They are written to be included in the language arts program. The projects help the students express themselves in a variety of manners, such as in written form, orally, and artistically.

The projects vary greatly and sometimes may even be coordinated with another part of the curriculum. The students may be asked to write a diary, a skit or play, a story, a conversation, a description, or a setting. There are also two pages that develop editing and revision skills in a step-by-step fashion.

The Teacher Pages:

The Procedures and Materials pages are included to help the teacher know how to prepare the students for the project and know what materials are needed for that project. The notes also suggest how the project can be done—whether alone, with a partner, or in a group.

The Student Pages:

The teacher chooses a project and then makes enough copies of the student page for the entire class. These pages take the student step-by-step through the project, from planning sessions all the way to completion. Usually, sample writings are given on each page to give students inspiration to develop their own ideas.

Procedures and Materials for Writing Projects

PAGE 10: AUTHORING FAIRY TALES

- Teachers, you may wish to read a few short fairy tales or discuss some fairy tales to begin this project.
- Discussion of the elements of a fairy tale may be very helpful to the students before they begin their own.
- Students will need paper and pencils for the four parts of the assignment.
- They may need computer time, if possible, in case they want to type their final drafts.
- Markers, crayons, or colored pencils will be needed to illustrate their tales.

PAGE 11: AUTOBIOGRAPHIES

- Teachers, you may wish to read short excerpts from a few autobiographies to give the students some ideas about how to begin. You may want to lead a discussion of major events that happened in their own lives that they may want to share.
- Another discussion about what students hope for their futures could also be helpful for the second part of their stories.
- Perhaps they could share some people in their lives that meant a great deal to them.
- They may need computer time in case they want to type their final drafts.

PAGE 12: BEAUTY AND THE BEAST

- Students are to be placed with a partner or in a small group for this project.
- They need paper and pencil to write a play based on "Beauty and the Beast."
- They will assign parts of their plays to members of the group, memorize the parts, and present their plays for the class.
- They may want to bring in costumes and props for their performances.
- They may even use old bed sheets to make a backdrop for their plays if time permits.
- They will need a day to perform their plays.

PAGE 13: BIOGRAPHIES

- Students should be teamed with a partner for this project.
- They will need paper and pencil for their interviews.
- The teacher may lead a discussion of possible questions they could ask their partners about their lives.
- Finally, they should be regrouped with four or six students who are partners so they can share the biographies that they wrote about their partners.

PAGE 14: BOOK CRITIQUE

- A week or two before beginning this project, students will be placed with a partner to read a book to each other for 15 or 20 minutes each day (this is necessary to complete the project).
- Together, the two partners will be writing a fictional interview with the author of the book they have read. One of the partners will play the author, and the second partner will play the interviewer.
- After they have written the script, they can memorize their parts and perform the interviews for the class.
- If possible, the interviews could be recorded with a video recorder or digital recorder.

PAGE 15: BOOK REPORT CHOICES

- It may be a good idea to take a poll of the kind of book report each student chooses after the teacher gives them the student sheet listing the book report choices.
- The teacher then gathers the materials needed. In most cases, poster board will be needed. Art paper will be needed if the students choose to make comic books or comic strips.
- They will need paper and pencils for their first drafts and markers to color their illustrations if they choose the comic book, poster, or comic strip.

Procedures and Materials for Writing Projects

PAGE 16: BOOK REPORT MOBILES

- Students will need paper and pencils to write the parts of their book reports.
- Each student needs to have at least six 5″ by 8″ index cards.
- They will each need a large poster upon which they will glue the parts of the book report.
- They also need markers to draw pictures on the back of each section.
- Yarn and paper punches will be needed to make the holes where they will string the yarn through so the mobiles can be hung.

PAGE 19: CHARACTERS FROM VARIOUS POINTS OF VIEW

- The students will write four selections for this project.
- Each description will be describing just one person from the view of four different aquaintances.
- As an example, they could describe Cinderella as seen by: the mice in her room, one of the stepsisters, the prince, and her stepmother.
- They will then write each of the descriptions on art paper, which they will fold to make a kind of brochure that they will illustrate.
- They will need a day to share their brochures.

PAGE 17: CATHEDRAL MYSTERY

- This is a good lesson if you will be studying the Middle Ages, but it is good any time. Each student will need a large piece of poster board and then a colored piece of paper to go on top of the poster board.
- They will be making a kind of "Advent Calendar" where there are little windows to open.
- The students will write their stories inside the windows after the colored cathedral is glued down to the poster, **OR** they may write their stories on the poster and then cut windows out of the top sheet, showing the parts of the story.

PAGE 20: CINDERELLA

- The students will have to be grouped in groups of three or four.
- They will assign one person of the group to be the recording secretary.
- They will brainstorm many ideas for a story based on the "Cinderella" theme.
- The secretary will record all the ideas.
- They will discuss all the ideas and decide on an outline of a story.
- They will divide the story into sections and either give each member a section to write, or they may write the section with a partner.
- They will come together and share what they wrote and critique each other's writing.

PAGE 18: CHARACTERS FROM A CHILD'S POINT OF VIEW

- Students will need paper and pencils to write their descriptions of ONE person as seen through the eyes of five different children.
- They will need markers, crayons, or colored pencils to draw each character (it will be the same character as seen in five different ways).
- They will need a day to share the character descriptions and to show the class their illustrations.

PAGE 21: COMIC BOOK HEROES

- For this project, each student will need two pieces of a heavier stock paper measuring 9″ by 12″.
- They will design four characters for their comic book stories: two good characters, a villain, and a victim.
- They will write short stories involving their characters.
- They can follow the diagrams on their student sheets to make their books.
- They will illustrate each section in the larger rectangles and print their text in the smaller ones as shown on the student page.

Procedures and Materials for Writing Projects

PAGE 22: CONFLICT RESOLUTION

- Before beginning this project, teachers may want to lead a discussion of events that happen in school, on the school bus, in the cafeteria, or in neighborhoods that can get out of control and lead to a serious conflict.
- Divide the students into groups of three or four for this project. The assignment is to develop a play showing a conflict that arises and how they would diffuse the situation.
- Each student must have a part in the play.
- They will write their plays, memorize their parts, and perform their plays for the class.
- A good follow-up activity would be for the class to discuss alternative ways to bring peace to the situation.

PAGE 23: DESCRIBING A TEENAGER

- Students must have a partner to complete this project.
- They will design and write a detailed description of five imaginary teenagers.
- There is to be no dialogue in the descriptions, just how they look, act, walk, stand, and their general demeanor.
- On the assigned day, they will act out each of the descriptions with no spoken words, like a mime.
- They may use costumes if they wish.
- The class may then comment on characteristics they observed in each character.

PAGE 24: DESCRIBING CHARACTERS FROM AN EXTERIOR VIEWPOINT

- The students will write <u>very</u> detailed descriptions of five people as if they are standing right next to them and the people are unable to see them.
- They will circle the person and then describe what they see.
- Each student will choose his/her best character, and on the assigned day, either present the memorized description or read it to the class.
- They may also want to use costumes or props.

PAGE 25: DESIGNING CHARACTERS

- For this project, each student will develop two or three characters in an organized manner as suggested on the student page.
- After they have designed these characters, they will write a story involving some or all of the characters.
- Finally, they may illustrate one or all of the characters.
- If time permits, each student can share a character description and the illustration with the class.

PAGE 26: DESIGNING SETTINGS

- To begin this project, it may be a good idea if you go over the detailed definition of "setting" as it is given on the student page.
- Students will work alone to complete this project.
- They can begin by brainstorming to make a chart like the one on the student page listing a possible "time," "place," and "environment" for their settings.
- Then they will write four short settings, choose their favorite, and write a story including the setting.
- Each student will need a piece of poster board and markers to complete the project.
- Finally, they will place their stories and colored illustrations on posters and share them with the class.

PAGE 27: DR. JEKYLL AND MR. HYDE

- For this project, it may be good to review the actual story of *Dr. Jekyll and Mr. Hyde* with the students.
- They will then write entries for a diary, and these entries will include entries made by both Dr. Jekyll and Mr. Hyde.
- They will place their entries on paper the size of a diary (about 4″ by 6″) and make a stiff cover for the diary. They could possibly cover that stiff cover with cloth or wrinkled brown paper to make it look very old and authentic or leathery.

Procedures and Materials for Writing Projects

PAGE 28: EDITING YOUR WRITING

- This project page is the only one that has a partner page. It is called "Revising Your Writing" and is located on page 45 in this book.
- This page on editing should probably be done before doing page 45.
- The students will only need a colored pen or fine-point marker to make the corrections in the story on the student sheet, using the editing symbols shown on the student page.
- You can then make another more lengthy assignment that they will do for the remainder of the week.
- This is a good lesson to use when the students have a specific story to write.

PAGE 31: GHOST STORY

- To prepare the students for this project, it may be good to read a few short ghost stories.
- They will then write ghost stories of their own.
- They will need to be placed in small groups to share their first drafts.
- They will need time to write their final drafts and possibly type them on a computer.
- They will need art paper, paintbrushes, and paint with which to paint their ghosts or haunted houses.
- They will need a day set aside to share their stories and pictures.

PAGE 29: EXTERNAL CONFLICT

- Students will work with a partner to complete this project.
- The play will involve two characters who are faced with a problem from the exterior or from an external situation.
- They will memorize their parts and then, on an assigned day, perform their play for the class.
- They may choose to bring costumes and props the day of the presentation.
- Their classmates will try to identify the conflict that the players are attempting to reveal.

PAGE 32: THE GRASS IS ALWAYS GREENER

- The students will first write about three characters who are dissatisfied with their lives, or they see someone else's life as better than theirs.
- Each student will choose his/her best character and write a news story as if he/she were a reporter for a newspaper.
- On an appointed day, each student will sit at a desk in front of the class and report the story as if he/she were a television reporter. (Students may read the reports or memorize them.)

PAGE 30: FOLKTALE RETELLING

- To begin this project, it might be a good idea to spend a couple of days reading some folktales to the students. There are folktales the world over, so they are easy to find.
- The students then will have to have some library time to research, so they can find a folktale they want to retell in their own words.
- After they write their folktales, they will memorize them and tell them to the class, as if they were traveling storytellers.
- They may wear costumes, and this is a good lesson to videotape, if possible.
- Finally, the class will make kindly suggestions and/or comments to the students about their performances.

PAGE 33: INTERNAL CONFLICT

- It may be a good idea to discuss some types of internal conflicts other than the examples given on the student page.
- Everyone experiences internal conflict or stress about something in their lives.
- The students each write a story about someone experiencing internal conflict.
- Finally, they will need art paper to illustrate or make several illustrations of their characters experiencing these conflicts.

Procedures and Materials for Writing Projects

PAGE 34: KLUTZ FINDS KLUTZ

- Students will write a fictional story about a klutzy friend of theirs.
- The friend (the klutz) would like this person to somehow introduce him/her to another person who is also a klutz.
- Before the students begin this lesson, it may be a good idea to brainstorm with the class about the different ways in which two people can meet. (They can be introduced, they can "bump" into each other, they can place an ad in the newspaper, etc.)
- The students will need part of a poster board to write their stories and to illustrate the two klutzes.

PAGE 37: MAGICAL HAT

- For this project, the students will need to be placed with partners or in small groups.
- They will design four or five fantastic hats, each with a magical ability.
- Then, each person will take the four or five hat designs and write a selection involving each hat.
- After writing their selections, they will come together to share their writings and get suggestions from their groups.
- They will then write the paragraphs in final form, and together, the students in the group will illustrate all the hats.
- They will share their hat designs and their stories on an assigned day.

PAGE 35: KNIGHT SAVES DAMSEL IN DISTRESS

- This is a good lesson to integrate with the study of the Middle Ages, but it is a good writing lesson at any time of the year.
- Each student will pretend to be a traveling newsperson or courier from the Middle Ages who has come to tell a daring tale of the rescue of a maiden in trouble.
- The students will need paper and pencils to write their first drafts.
- They will need long strips of paper to make scrolls, perhaps 12″ by 20″ for their final drafts.
- On the assigned day, they may read their accounts in a dramatic manner.
- They may choose to wear costumes, also.

PAGE 38: MAKING A CLASSROOM NEWSPAPER

- The students should be divided into small groups for this assignment.
- They will need paper and pencils to write the newspaper articles and markers to color their pictures.
- They will brainstorm the kinds of articles they want in their newspapers.
- If they want to interview another student, a teacher, or the principal, they should make an appointment to do so. They may have to miss class time to keep their appointments. (This will be entirely up to you to decide.)
- Large pieces of heavier stock paper should be provided, upon which to print and illustrate the newspapers.

PAGE 36: LEGENDS

- The students will need to have some time to research legendary characters in the library. After they have read about some of these characters, they will write short skits involving the legendary character of their choice.
- They may include two, three, or four persons who interact in their stories.
- If time permits, they could perform their skits after gathering volunteers to play the parts of each person.

PAGE 39: MAPPING YOUR FANTASY

- Each student will work alone to make a large map of either a place he/she is reading about or has read about in a book or a place he/she makes up entirely in his/her imagination.
- They will each need a poster board and many colored markers or crayons to color their maps.
- They should have knowledge of map keys and how they are made up, because they will make map keys for their fantasy maps.
- Finally, on an assigned day, they may share their maps.

Procedures and Materials for Writing Projects

PAGE 40: ONOMATOPOEIA

- The students will make a brochure this week that advertises a noisy machine, amusement park ride, vehicle, or any other sound- or noise-producing item.
- They will write detailed descriptions of the item they choose to "advertise" in their brochures.
- They will all need a sheet of art paper measuring 8 1/2″ by 11″, folding it into thirds like a brochure.
- They will illustrate the covers with their noisy things and print their descriptions on the inside of the brochures.

PAGE 43: RAGS TO RICHES

- The students will work with partners to develop stories of someone who is really down-and-out.
- Then they will hand their stories in to you. You will choose the most promising stories, or you may choose to have all of the partners develop their stories into plays.
- The project can end here, or the pairs of students who have written these plays can then try to produce the plays using their classmates as actors.

PAGE 41: PIZZAZZY PARTS OF SPEECH

- To begin this project, students should have a very clear idea of the basic parts of speech: nouns, verbs, prepositions, adverbs, and adjectives.
- They should be assigned to small groups of three or four persons.
- Each group is supplied strips of lined chart paper that has been cut in half lengthwise.
- They will label each sheet as shown on the student page.
- They will list as many parts of speech as they can on each sheet, and they should print each word about one inch high.
- They will then hang all their lists around the room or on the chalkboard and follow the student page directions for the rest of the project.

PAGE 44: REGULAR GUY OR GIRL BECOMES A HERO

- Each student will work with a partner to write a newspaper article about a regular kid doing something VERY courageous and becoming a hero.
- They will need a large piece of posterboard to use like the front page of a newspaper.
- They can print out their article on the computer and cut and paste it to the poster, or they can just print right on the poster board.
- They can then make an illustration of their hero on the poster.

PAGE 42: PRODUCING A STORYBOARD

- Students will work with partners to write short stories.
- Then they will produce storyboards developed from those stories.
- Each set of partners will need one-half of a sheet of posterboard to make the storyboard.
- They will need markers or crayons to color the illustrations.
- They may need computer time if they want to type the text below each illustration, or they may print it by hand.

PAGE 45: REVISING YOUR WRITING

- This page is a good one to use after the students have completed page 28 of this book, which is called "Editing Your Writing."
- The students will need paper, pencils, and colored pens or fine markers to rewrite the story on the student page.
- After they have revised or REWRITTEN the page, they will write entirely new stories. Then they will edit and revise them, and then edit the stories again.
- Finally, they will write final drafts that are, hopefully, perfect.

Procedures and Materials for Writing Projects

PAGE 46: ROBIN HOOD

- Students will work with a partner to complete this project.
- For this project, students should have a fairly clear idea of the Robin Hood stories. Perhaps you could read a few chapters of a "Robin Hood" book before beginning the project.
- They will need paper and pencils and at least a 9″ by 12″ piece of art paper or poster board, along with markers or crayons.
- They will be making a "Wanted" poster announcing the crimes committed by Robin Hood and his Merry Men.
- Finally, they will choose an idea from the box on the right of the student page and complete the second part of the project.

PAGE 49: SETTINGS

- This week, the students will work alone to write four settings.
- It may be a good idea to read a few good written settings to the students before they begin.
- The settings they write should be very detailed and descriptive.
- After they complete their settings, they will need to have a piece of posterboard.
- They will divide their poster into four sections, and they will illustrate all four settings on the poster.
- On the assigned day, they will share their writings and posters with the class.

PAGE 47: ROMEO AND JULIET

- The students may work with a partner or alone to complete this project.
- The story they write will be either a monologue or a dialogue written from the viewpoint of someone who actually knew the couple, like Romeo or Juliet's mother or father or one of their brothers or sisters.
- After they have written the piece, they will memorize their parts and perform the work for the class on an appointed day.

PAGE 50: TALL TALE CHARACTERS

- This week, each student will invent a new tall tale character.
- To begin, it would be a good idea to read some tall tales to the students, or perhaps they could all read a tall tale story a week or two before beginning this project.
- Research could be done in the library to search for tall tale characters.
- They will write a story including a **NEW** tall tale character.
- They will all need two or three long strips of paper to print their story.
- They will illustrate a cover for their story.

PAGE 48: SCIENCE FICTION WEEK

- The students will work alone to complete a science fiction piece.
- It may be a good idea to discuss the elements of a science fiction story before they begin.
- Usually, there is some kind of alien invasion, and the aliens usually want to take over our planet or bodies because their own planet is endangered.
- The Earth people always put up a valiant fight to regain their planet, and they usually win.
- Perhaps it would be a good idea to discuss some science fiction movies before they begin writing.
- Finally, they will share the story with a group.

PAGE 51: TOY STORIES

- For this project, students will design five toys that in some magical manner come to life and have an adventure.
- They will choose one or more toy characters, and they will write a story involving this character or characters.
- They will finally make either an illustration or an actual replica of their toy. On the assigned day, they will share their story and illustration or toy replica with the class or a small group.

Procedures and Materials for Writing Projects

PAGE 52: TRUTH IN ADVERTISING

- To complete this project, students have to watch at least one hour of television.
- They will pay attention to the commercials within the program.
- They will take notes about exactly what is "CLAIMED" by each product being advertised.
- They may have to watch more than an hour to get enough statements that they can record.
- They can watch television on their own or with their group, whatever you decide.
- After they have gathered all the "CLAIMS" made by a certain product, they will come together to categorize the statements on a poster as shown on the student page.

PAGE 55: WRITING DESCRIPTIONS

- The objective for this project is that students write about the assigned topic with great detail.
- The first thing they will describe is a person whom they know very well.
- The second description they will write is for a very familiar object.
- The third thing they will write about is a fictional character, some character in a story or a place, or a space alien (other things are suggested on the student page).
- The fourth thing they will describe is how to do something with which they are familiar, like how to play a soccer game or Monopoly™.

PAGE 53: UGLY DUCKLING

- Students will work with a small group to develop a story and then a storyboard based on the story "The Ugly Duckling."
- It may be a good idea to read the original story to the class before they begin their own story.
- They will need paper and pencil to complete this, and they also need one-half of a sheet of posterboard cut lengthwise.
- They will illustrate each block and either type their text and then cut and paste it to the poster, or they can print it by hand on the poster.
- They will present their storyboard to the class or a small group, and the group will make kindly suggestions.

PAGE 56: WRITING FABLES

- This week, the students will be writing their own fables.
- To begin this project, it might be a good idea if you could read a few fables to the students, like "The Tortoise and the Hare" and have a discussion of the lesson that is taught by each fable.
- Then the students will work alone to develop their own fables that have hidden morals or lessons.
- They will each need three sheets of paper measuring 10″ wide by 6″ high. They will fold the paper in half to make a small book, as shown on the student page.

PAGE 54: WRITING A TELEPHONE CONVERSATION

- To complete this project, students will be placed with a partner, and together they will write a script for a telephone conversation.
- The conversation may be with a good friend or someone you do not know at all and are speaking to for the first time.
- Make the conversation interesting, and, if at all possible, have your characters be somewhat mysterious.
- After the scripts are completed, the students will share their scripts with the class.

PAGE 57: WRITING FROM ANOTHER POINT OF VIEW

- This week, the students will write a story with which they are familiar, for example, "Cinderella," from the point of view of another character in the story, like the fairy godmother. Perhaps they could retell "Peter Pan" from the viewpoint of Wendy or Tinkerbell.
- After they have written their story, they will memorize it and present it to the class as if they were a traveling storyteller.
- If they are really motivated, they may wear costumes and bring props.

Procedures and Materials for Writing Projects

PAGE 58: WRITING FUN WITH IDIOMS

- It may be a good idea to begin this project with a brainstorming session on idioms that are frequently used in everyday conversation.
- The students will work with a partner to write a story using as many idioms as they can within the story.
- The story can sound pretty goofy and should be lots of fun to write.
- After they finish their stories, they can share them either with the class or a small group.

PAGE 59: WRITING SCARY STORIES

- For this project, students work alone to write four assignments:
  - a. a flow chart;
  - b. a character web;
  - c. a first draft; and
  - d. a final draft of a scary story.
- They will need two pieces of lined chart paper to make their flow chart and their character webs.
- When they finish their work, you may want them to share their work with the class.

PAGE 60: WRITING SONG LYRICS

- This week, students will work with a partner to write new lyrics for three common songs.
- After they write them, they will print each song on three large pieces of chart paper. The letters should be at least one inch tall.
- On the assigned day, the partners will put their charts on the chalkboard or wall with tape.
- They may want to sing their new songs for the class or have the whole class join in to sing the songs with them.

NCTE Standard for Language Arts: Students use a wide range of strategies to communicate for a variety of purposes

Authoring Fairy Tales

ASSIGNMENTS AND GUIDELINES:

This week, we will be writing a new fairy tale. Before you begin, it may help you to think of the many fairy tales you have read in the past. Your assignments are as follows:

1. When the entire assignment is completed, you will hand in four parts:
   a. a list of characters and character descriptions
      1. a hero or heroine
      2. a victim or victims
      3. a villain or villains
   b. a general description of a plot for your story
   c. an outline of your fairy tale (a sample of an outline is written on the right)
   d. a final draft of your fairy tale with illustrations

Here are some samples of possible characters:

1. Hero: Horace the mouse, a tiny little gray mouse with very large ears, who lives in an enormous mansion, in a dollhouse, with his owner.
2. Victim: Shanell is a lonely young girl, who lives with her parents in the mansion and is cared for by the wicked nanny Felonia.
3. Villain: A witch in disguise as a nanny, Felonia is a tall, skinny woman who appears to be a perfect nanny until she is left alone with Shanell. Then she does dreadful things to torture her young charge, like locking her in a closet and feeding her only bread and milk.

Sample Outline:

1. Shanell, a shy girl with long straggly brown hair, lives in a 45-room mansion at the top of a large hill with her parents, Juan and Gladys.
2. Juan and Gladys are very busy globetrotters, and they are seldom home, so they hire a nanny to teach and care for Shanell.
3. The nanny, Felonia, is really a wicked witch disguised as a nanny. She is tall and bony with long black hair and huge black-rimmed glasses. She is very sweet with Shanell's parents, but horrid to Shanell.
4. Felonia locks Shanell in a closet each and every day, and feeds her only stale bread and milk.
5. Shanell tries to tell her parents about Felonia, but they shush her away and tell her to go to her room to play.
6. One day, when Shanell is in the dark closet, a small gray mouse comes under the door. He comes up to Shanell, offers her his paw in an elegant manner, and says, "How DO you do...my name is Horace, and may I ask YOUR name please...?

NCTE Standard for Language Arts: Students employ a wide range of strategies as they write and use different writing process elements appropriately to communicate with different audiences for a variety of purposes.

Autobiographies

ASSIGNMENTS AND GUIDELINES:

This week, you will be writing your autobiography, and you will do this in four steps.

1. First you will write 20 sentences about things in your **PAST** and **PRESENT** (10 sentences for each). These sentences do not have to be in chronological order, for they will act as a starting point for the final story you will write.
2. Then you will write seven to eight statements about your **FUTURE.** These can be things that you dream for or hope for when you are older.
3. Now you will write about the person or persons that you believe are the most important person(s) in your life. Tell about each of their personalities and how they affected you.
4. Now you will write your autobiography in final form. If you have time, make a cover for your piece with an illustration(s) on the front.
5. Be prepared to share your autobiography with your literary partner or group.

Sample "PAST" paragraph:

When I was two years old, my mom let my two aunts babysit me. These two aunts were only eight and nine years old at the time. Well, they put me in one of those old-fashioned buggies. You know, the ones with the hood that keeps the sun from your face. They decided to take me for a walk. After a time, they started to argue about whose turn it was to push the buggy. At that moment, they were at the top of a hill, and before they knew what was happening, the buggy started moving rapidly down the sidewalk. Well, thank goodness, it turned over on its side, and I was plopped onto the soft grass...

Sample "IMPORTANT PERSON" paragraph:

One person who has affected my life, I never even knew. It was my Uncle Johnny. He was my mom's older brother. When I was born, my uncle was in Europe because there was a war, and he was in the army. My mom sent him a letter with my baby picture in it, and he sent me a tiny, beautiful turquoise ring (because I was born in December). My mom said he couldn't wait to see me, and every letter that he wrote to her, spoke of me. But he never saw me. He died in the war, and when they found his body, my baby picture was in his pocket, next to his heart.

NCTE Standard for Language Arts: Students employ a wide range of strategies as they write and use different writing process elements appropriately to communicate with different audiences for a variety of purposes.

Beauty and the Beast

ASSIGNMENTS AND GUIDELINES:

This week, you will be working with one, two, or three other persons to write a script for a play that follows the literary theme of "Beauty and the Beast." You may make your "Beast" a real person who just acts like a beast, or you may make it a female, somewhat like the shrew in Shakespeare's "The Taming of the Shrew." You may choose to base your story on the "Frog Prince" in which the princess has to kiss the frog to change him into a prince. Your story may take place long ago, in the present, or in the future. Whatever you decide, be sure that you follow the storyline of the Beauty and the Beast idea. The guidelines for the week are listed below:

1. First, decide with your group what storyline you will use for the script.
2. Decide on the number of characters you want in the story.
3. Do some planning, whether it be a story map, a Venn Diagram, or an outline.
4. Write the script. Be sure to include which characters are on stage, off stage, where the characters stand, etc.
5. Decide on the set design or props you need, and assign duties to various people.
6. Assign parts to students, and memorize, practice, and, finally, perform the play for the class.
7. If time remains, perhaps you could critique the other groups' plays.

Sample Script Excerpt:

The setting is in New York City in the 1930s. The characters are a mother and her three children, Megan, age 17; Mark, age 7; and Roger, age 5. Their father died three years ago, leaving the family penniless. The mother works as a short-order cook down the street during the day, and at night, she works in an office building as a cleaning lady. Megan cannot attend school, because she stays home to watch her siblings. One day at the restaurant, her mother gets badly burned and can no longer work. Megan has to find work. She searches the want ads and finds an ad for a cook/cleaning person in a large brownstone private house in Manhattan. The play opens as Megan walks up the street with the ad in her hand. It is winter, and snow is falling:

Megan: "I guess this is the place. Wow, is it a big house!"
(Just then a gentleman comes out of the house next door.)

Neighbor: "Hello there, can I help you with something?"

Megan: "No thank you, I am just here to have an interview for a job position in this home"

Neighbor: "You have got to be kidding! You are going to work in the same house with that freak?"

Megan: "What are you talking about?"

Neighbor: "That 'GUY' in there is as ugly and weird as anyone could be. He never comes out of the house. Some people think he has a terrible past and that is why he doesn't ever show himself..."

NCTE Language Arts Standard: Students conduct research on issues and interests by generating ideas and questions and by posing problems.

BIOGRAPHIES

ASSIGNMENTS/GUIDELINES FOR THE WEEK:

For this lesson, you will be writing a biography of a partner assigned to you by your teacher. To do this, follow these instructions:

1. You will need several pieces of loose-leaf paper or your writing journal.
2. First, you will write 20 or more questions that you could ask your partner about his/her life. (Examples are on the right.)
3. Skip at least three spaces between each question to leave spaces for writing the answer your partner will give you.
4. After your questions have been written and checked by your teacher, you may interview your partner.
5. When the interview is complete, take the answers he/she has given you and begin putting them in some kind of order.
6. Write a biography about your partner, trying to keep it in a somewhat chronological or timely order.
7. Write or type a final draft of the story.
8. If you finish the piece and time remains, please make a cover for your biography with a portrait of the person.
9. Share the biography with your partner.

   * Be sure to make your questions ones that ask for a detailed answer. That way, your final biography will be more interesting. If your questions ask for broad, or general, answers, the final piece will not be as exciting.
10. Finally, share the biography with a small group and ask for questions or suggestions.

SAMPLE QUESTIONS:

Question: Where were you born: city, state, and hospital?
Answer: I was born in New Kensington, Pennsylvania, in Citizens General Hospital.

Question: When you were young, even before you can remember, what is something that happened to you that your mom told you about?
Answer: When I was two, my mom told me that I was playing with another kid, and we had little cups of juice. I got mad at the kid because he wanted my toy, so I poured my juice on his head.

Question: When you first went to school, how did you feel about it, and what was one memorable experience you had from the early years?
Answer: I did not want to go to school at all, so, on the first day of kindergarten, my mom had to drag me, screaming and kicking out of the house and onto the bus. When I got to school, I walked right back home! I remember that year also, taking a bottle of glue and gluing my hand to my desk!

NCTE Standard for Language Arts: Students employ a wide range of strategies as they write and use different writing process elements appropriately to communicate with different audiences for a variety of purposes.

BOOK CRITIQUE

ASSIGNMENTS AND GUIDELINES:

This week, you will work with an appointed partner to do the following:

1. You will choose a book you have just read from which you will develop a script that will be a staged interview.
2. One of you will play the part of a famous author. The second partner will play a famous interviewer or literary critic on television.
3. You will proceed to write the script surrounding the book you have chosen as the object of the interview.
4. You may choose to take opposing views of the book, just as movie critics take opposite views of a movie they have just seen, **or** you may wish to agree on the book in question. Whatever you do, please tell the basic story of the book as you write the script, and explain some of the exciting parts of the story.
5. When you complete your script, run through it, make the changes you think necessary, and make a final, flawless draft.
6. Memorize the script, gather costumes and props, if you like, then be prepared to enact the interview. If a camcorder or digital recorder is available, tape the interview.

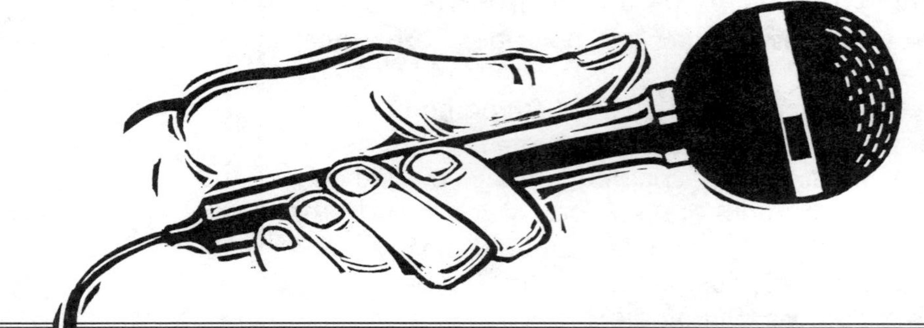

SUGGESTED QUESTIONS & RESPONSES:

QUESTION: Mr. Mark Twain, I read your books entitled *The Adventures of Tom Sawyer* and *The Adventures of Huckleberry Finn* when I was a young girl, and they deeply affected me. I particularly liked the character of Tom Sawyer. He was such an imp! Could you tell all our readers about this character and if you developed this person from someone you knew in your own childhood?

ANSWER: Well, Barbara, the character of Tom Sawyer was a fun character to write about, because he was such a mischievous one. I actually developed him because I was always making up stories in my mind, and his character just came to me one day. I knew many a boy in my young years who mirrored Tom.

QUESTION: Mr. Twain, I have heard that many of the adventures Tom Sawyer and Huck Finn have in the books are based on actual events in your own life. Is that true?

ANSWER: Actually, many of the tight spots the two boys got into were similar to events in my own childhood. I also had an aunt who inspired me for the character of Tom's Aunt Polly. She was very dear to me. I was mischievous like Tom. In fact, some may say I still have a little mischievousness in my delightful personality to this day!

NCTE Standard for Language Arts: Students employ a wide range of strategies as they write and use different writing process elements appropriately to communicate with different audiences for a variety of purposes.

BOOK REPORT CHOICES

ASSIGNMENTS AND GUIDELINES:

This week, you will be writing a book report about a book you have very recently read and one that is a favorite book that you would like to share with the class. You may choose from several formats on the right, or you may get permission to do another type of book report if you have a great idea for one. Whatever the format you choose, you must include the following information about your book.

1. The <u>title</u> of the book
2. The <u>author</u> and perhaps <u>illustrator</u> of the book
3. A list of the main <u>characters</u> and a brief description of these characters.
4. A <u>summary</u> of the storyline or plot (no more than 15 sentences)
5. The person(s) in our class whom you think would enjoy reading this book or a <u>recommendation</u> to a group
6. The reason you think the author wrote this book, otherwise known as: the <u>author's purpose</u>
7. How you think this <u>book will help you</u> in your life or how this book has helped you already

Here is a list of the various types of book reports you may choose to do this week. Choose the one you think would be interesting for you, then write out your book report following the format on the left of this page and put it into your chosen format:

1. You may do a book report "Commercial," just like the commercials on TV. For example:

"This is a news bulletin for all you mystery fans out there. Jenny Smith has just published her latest thriller-diller entitled *The Mystery of the Lost Island.* This is a book that finds Marcy and Tracy on a ship to an island in the Caribbean when a storm suddenly comes up and smashes the ship into the rocks. They suddenly find themselves the only survivors on an island with huge dinosaur creatures. They go from cave to cave, trying to avoid a confrontation with one of the creatures. On the second day after the wreck, they run into a cave, and lo and behold, there is a young boy there."

2. You may do a "Comic Strip" report. For example:

This is a picture of my main character, Tracy. She is a headstrong girl who seldom listens to anyone. She is very rich and spoiled...

This picture shows Marcy, Tracy's best friend. Marcy always lets Tracy get her own way in everything because she is afraid of losing her friendship...

3. You may do a "Comic Book" book report. For example:

picture of shipwreck	picture of Tracy & Marcy	picture of the boy in a cave
explanation of pictures		explanation of boy and cave
picture of island	picture of caves	picture of one of the creatures
explanation of pictures		explanation of creature behavior

4. You may also make a book report "Poster":

The Mystery of the Lost Island
By Jenny Smith

CHARACTERS: Tracy Plitt, a spoiled rich girl from Manhattan and an heiress of the Windemere Foundation. She is a spoiled, haughty girl who orders her friends around. The only friend she has remaining is Marcy, the other main character of the story. Marcy is a kind, gentle person who believes that Tracy is arrogant because of a lack of attention...

picture goes here

PLOT: The story begins on a ship headed to an island. A terrible storm slams the ship into rocks, and it sinks... Tracy and Marcy are stranded on an island filled with giant creatures that look like they are from the Jurassic Period. They hide in caves for a day and night, and then...

NCTE Language Arts Standard: Students use spoken, written, and visual language to accomplish their own purposes (e.g., for learning, enjoyment, persuasion, and the exchange of information).

BOOK REPORT MOBILES

ASSIGNMENTS AND GUIDELINES:

This week you will be doing THREE things. First, you will write a first draft of a book report that is broken into sections. You will then write each of these sections on large index cards (5″ x 8″) and glue each card to a piece of poster board (to make it stronger). You will then cut each of the cards out of the poster board and you will arrange the sections together to form a mobile like the one to the right. Here is a list of the parts of the book report you should have:

a. the title of the book
b. the author and/or illustrator
c. descriptions of each of the two or three main characters of the book
d. a summary of the book
e. your favorite part
f. the author's purpose for writing the book

1. To begin, write the first draft of the parts of your book report on looseleaf paper.
2. Print each section on index cards.
3. On the back of each card, draw something that is symbolic from your story.
4. Color the poster board illustration with markers.
5. Punch holes about 1 cm from the edge of your poster board pieces, then string them together with yarn as shown to the right.
6. Perhaps your teacher or teacher's helper can hang them from the ceiling to celebrate a literature event.

A Sample Book Report Mobile:

Jan's Journey to Jupiter
written by Jill North and illustrated by Paul Ramos

Character - Jan Romi
Jan has been assigned to the secret mission of going to Jupiter, because Earth has lost touch with our colony there. She is an expert in such things.

Character- Petrus
Petrus is a guard who lives at the entrance to the space dome on Jupiter. He is a kind alien who has been imported to Jupiter from the moon, Io.

SUMMARY:
After hearing of the lack of communication from the Jupiter Colony, Jan is assigned to go there to investigate. She and her small crew land...

FAVORITE PART/AUTHOR'S PURPOSE
My favorite part was when Jan first got to the Colony gate, she was standing there in her space-suit surrounded by swirling gases shouting for someone's response, and then out of the darkness...

THIS SHOWS THE BACK OF THE MOBILE

NCTE Language Arts Standard: Students draw on their prior experience, their research skills, and their interactions with other readers and writers.

Cathedral Mystery

ASSIGNMENTS & GUIDELINES:

1. You will write a mystery that is set inside a gothic cathedral. Some suggestions for a story are in the last column. You may choose to have your story take place in the Middle Ages when many cathedrals were built.
2. Edit and revise the story so it is without error.
3. Design a large cathedral that has lots of windows, something like the illustration to the right, because you will be cutting each window open and folding it back like a shutter or a door.
4. You will glue your cathedral on another piece of white paper. Then you will write your story in each window, paragraph by paragraph.
5. When you have finished your cathedral, if time remains, color your design.
6. Be prepared to share your cathedral and the story you wrote within its windows with the class.

SUGGESTIONS:

1. Your story could begin the day you visited the cathedral with your class and got lost in the basement of the cathedral where all the bishops are buried. The bus leaves without you, the cathedral is closed for the night, and there you are, all alone...
2. Your story could take place in the future when you are the Commander of Detectives for the Paris Police Department. A rash of robberies has been taking place in the Cathedral of Notre Dame. You have uncovered clues that point to a young child who is seen each day going into the cathedral. You have decided to spend the afternoon as an undercover policeman or as a homeless person, to see what you can see.
3. If you choose to have your story take place in the Middle Ages, you could be a young boy who is always getting into mischief. One day your mother chases you from the house with a broom for dropping her fresh bread dough on your little sister's head. You run off to the cathedral to see if you can find your friend Martin, when you see a man climbing down from the lowest window of the cathedral with a gold cup in his hand. You are very frightened, but you decide to try to trip him. You run after him, and as he turns, you see that it is your own father!

NCTE Standard for Language Arts: Students adjust their use of spoken, written, and visual language (e.g., conventions, style, vocabulary) to communicate effectively with a variety of audiences and for different purposes.

Characters from a Child's Point of View

ASSIGNMENTS AND GUIDELINES:

This week, you will be writing about one person as seen through the eyes of five very different children. YOU, the writer, will be pretending to be these five different children, and you will write detailed descriptions of the person you develop. You may have to carefully plan the person who is going to be described, or you may choose a famous character or a person who appeals to children. For the character whom the children are describing, an example may be Santa Claus, as seen from the viewpoint of a tough, eight-year-old bully who has grown up on the streets of the Bronx. Santa could also be seen by a delicate, young seven-year-old girl who has been ill since birth. A four-year-old boy who lives in a mansion and a four-year-old boy who lives in a trailer in a small town in Nebraska could also describe Santa. The final description could be from a five-year-old girl, who lives in a row house in a small town outside of Pittsburgh, PA. These are just some suggestions.

Your assignments are as follows:

1. You are to choose a character whom you will describe.
2. You will write at least one long paragraph describing the character as seen by each child (five paragraphs).
3. You will then illustrate the character, as seen by each child, on the paper provided.
4. You will share the illustrations and explain each.

SAMPLE DESCRIPTIONS:

Santa is described by a bully from the Bronx:

Oh man, you're asking me if I think Santa is coming to town. Give me a break! It's all a bunch of baloney! The only Santa I know is the guys who hang out with me. They get me food and a place to sleep. Nobody gives anybody nuthin' around here. Oh, yeah, there's those goodie-two-shoes that hand out hot potatoes on Christmas Eve and stuff, but that's only one night. Brother, it ain't no hot potato keepin' me warm the other nights of the winter! Where's Santa when there's an ache deep in my belly cause I'm so hungry? Where is he?

Four-year-old living in a mansion describing Santa:

Santa? Well I know Santa is a great old guy that I visit in Bloomingdale's every year. He really lives in the North Pole, you know. My nanny has taken me to see him every single year since I was a kid. All I know is, every single thing I have ever asked him for, I find right under my Christmas tree. He must have some kind of direct fax line to my dad. Last year, I got about a zillion presents! It took me till dinner time to open them all. Yes-sir-ree, I've gotten every single thing I've asked Santa for. Well, almost everything. I did ask him to help Mama come back, but she didn't.

NCTE Standard for Language Arts: Students adjust their use of spoken, written, and visual language (e.g., conventions, style, vocabulary) to communicate effectively with a variety of audiences and for different purposes.

Characters From Various Points of View

ASSIGNMENTS AND GUIDELINES:

This week, you will be writing about ONE particular character as seen by four different people. Of course, these four people will feel differently about this character. Just for an example: Imagine that a person chooses "Cinderella" as their character to describe. The persons describing her could be: 1. the prince, 2. the wicked stepmother, 3. the fairy godmother, and finally, 4. one of the mice that lives in the attic with her. These three persons (and a mouse) would, no doubt, see Cinderella very differently and have unique experiences with her.

Your assignments are as follows this week:

1. You are to choose <u>one</u> character whom you will either make up entirely or with whom you are very familiar in literature. (For example, some literary figures are: Romeo and Juliet, Hamlet, Macbeth, Julius Caesar, Santa Claus, Cinderella, or Paul Bunyan.
2. You will then choose the four characters who know your character, or think they do, and begin writing detailed descriptions, one from each of their viewpoints. Be sure to include both physical and emotional characteristics.
3. After you have completed the four descriptions, you will use the art paper provided for you by your teacher to make a brochure, writing the various viewpoints on each side. Be sure to illustrate your character from each of these persons' points of view.
4. Be prepared to share your brochures with the class.

IDEAS AND SUGGESTIONS:

From the viewpoint of Charlie Briggs, an Oklahoma City private investigator:

Maggie Marshall killed him in cold blood. I know she did. Let me tell you why I believe this to be true. One night about a year ago, Maggie and the deceased, Jimmy Smith, went out for a night on the town. Well, as they were going down Route 76, leading into Oklahoma City, they saw this hitchhiker standing by the road. Maggie insisted they pick her up. Well, they all became great friends, and one thing led to another, and the next thing you know, Jimmy is falling for the hitchhiker, and Maggie is left out in the cold...

From the viewpoint of Maggie's mother, Margaret Jamison:

My darling little girl would not hurt a fly. You have to believe me. I know there are times when she acts spoiled and haughty, but inside, she was a cream puff. What I think ruined her life was that no-good Jimmy Smith, and I'm glad he's dead! Why, my Maggie went to all the best schools and was in the Miss Oklahoma beauty pageant. She would have won if that rotten Charlie Briggs had not stirred up that trouble about Maggie cheating in college...

NCTE Standard for Language Arts: Students employ a wide range of strategies as they write and use different writing process elements appropriately to communicate with different audiences for a variety of purposes.

CINDERELLA

SOME BACKGROUND INFORMATION:

This week you will be writing a story based on the old favorite, "Cinderella." As you develop your characters, remember the following about that age-old story:

1. Cinderella was originally a very happy girl until her father remarried.
2. After her father died, she was treated as a slave by both her stepmother and her stepsisters.
3. They tried to make her very unhappy and break her spirit, but Cinderella remained an optimistic, loving person.
4. They found out that the king's son was looking for a wife and would hold an event that would bring all the eligible females to him.
5. The stepmother and stepsisters let Cinderella think she was going to the event, but then they tricked her into staying home.
6. Cinderella manages to attend the event, with help from her Fairy Godmother. But things don't go as expected, and she has to leave suddenly.
7. The prince finds her and they live happily...

ASSIGNMENTS AND GUIDELINES:

You will work with a cooperative group to write a story following the literary theme of a Cinderella story. Your assignments are as follows:

1. You will do some planning before you begin the story.
   a. Brainstorm for ideas, and have the secretary of your group write ALL the ideas down.
   b. Use either a Venn diagram or a word web to plan the characters.
2. Begin to write the story, break the group into pairs, and assign each pair of students a different aspect of the story.
3. Finally, each group will exchange the parts of the story they wrote, then put them together and share the whole story with the entire group. The group will critique the story.

NCTE Standard for Language Arts: Students employ a wide range of strategies as they write and use different writing process elements appropriately to communicate with different audiences for a variety of purposes.

COMIC BOOK HEROES

ASSIGNMENTS AND GUIDELINES:

This week you will be designing comic book heroes and writing a story about your characters. Then you will actually make a small comic book and place your text in the book. If you read comic books at all, you will know that comic book heroes are magical, super-human beings.

1. Your assignment is to design four characters for your comic book. Two good characters, a helpless victim, and one very evil comic book villain.
2. Make up a special power that each of your characters has, like being able to bite through steel or some other amazing ability.
3. The evil enemy has to have special powers of some kind, also.
4. Develop a story of how they all come together, with the very good heroes rescuing the victim from the dirty rotten villain—something like modern day knights.
5. Your job, therefore, is to design <u>two superheroes</u>, <u>one weak or helpless person</u>, and <u>one rotten, cruel villain</u>. Then follow the directions in the box to the right.

MAKING YOUR COMIC BOOK:

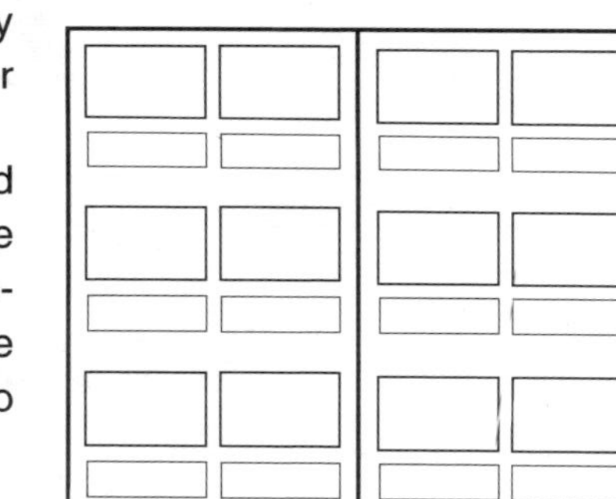

1. After you design the four characters for the comic book, write a story with your characters as the stars.
2. Divide the text into 24 little sections, one section of the text for each frame or each picture in the book.
3. Obtain two or three large pieces of heavy stock paper measuring about 9″ by 12″. Fold these two or three sheets in half to make the comic book.
4. Save one side for the cover. Divide the inside surface of each page into six sections. (These are just guides. You may have more or fewer of the sections for the pictures and text.)
5. Draw the pictures in the boxes, and place the text for each picture under the picture. You may want to have word bubbles instead of writing the text under the picture. After you complete the inside, do the cover illustration!
6. Be prepared to share your creation.

NCTE Standard for Language Arts: Students draw on their prior experience, their interactions with other readers and writers, their knowledge of word meaning and of other texts.

CONFLICT RESOLUTION

ASSIGNMENTS AND GUIDELINES:

This week, and possibly part of next week, you will be working in a group to write, produce, direct, and act in a play that you will write together. You will write a play that presents some aspects of "Conflict Resolution." As you know, one of the major problems in schools is that disagreements often snowball into complicated situations.

1. You will first develop an idea for a play. Where do you want your story to take place, what situation leads to the conflict that you will portray?
2. Now it is time to talk about the plot of your play. Remember, this is the problem that arises and the process that leads to the solution of the problem.
3. Thirdly, you will write the play. Be sure to include at least one part for each person in the group. Each person may play more than one part.
4. Finally, gather the props you need, memorize and practice your parts, and enact your play for the class. You may find it valuable if the class discusses each conflict and finds alternative resolutions for the conflict(s) in your play.

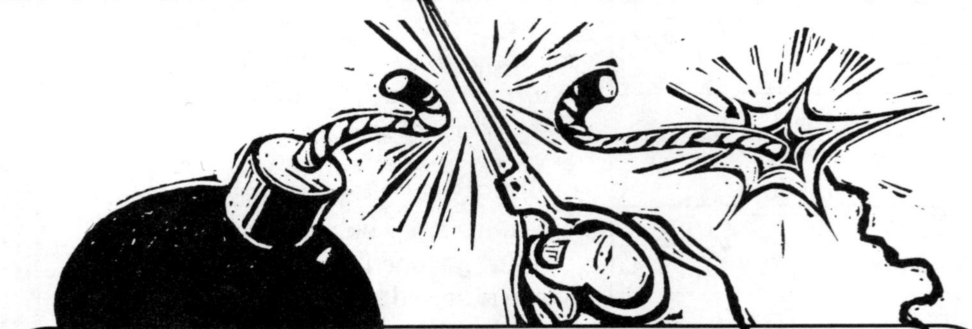

IDEAS FOR A SCRIPT:

Here are a few situations that you might use as a basis for your plot:

1. You are in the cafeteria having lunch with a group of your friends. A person known to be a school bully decides to sit down with your group. He's twice as big and strong as any of you. He tries to pick a fight with one of your friends. How would you handle this problem?
2. You are a girl in seventh grade on the first day of school. As you walk down the hall for the first time with a friend, a group of girls make snide remarks about the way you both look, the clothes you wear, and your hair. What can you do to change this situation peacefully?
3. One of your <u>best</u> friends is having trouble with math. She asks you to study with her, but then, at the study session, says that she will pay you five dollars for each set of homework answers that you give her. What will you do?

NCTE Standard for Language Arts: Students employ a wide range of strategies as they write and use different writing process elements appropriately to communicate with different audiences for a variety of purposes.

DESCRIBING A TEENAGER

ASSIGNMENTS AND GUIDELINES:

This week, you will be writing very detailed descriptions of teenagers who are about your age. You will work with a partner to do this. The following lists your assignments for the week:

1. You will design five different teenagers between the two of you.
2. Your approach to this assignment will be to write only about the physical appearance of these persons—the way they walk, sit, and stand. You will also write about their actions, for example, how they approach a classroom or enter a party. You will not include any dialogue. You will write as if you are an invisible person watching them.
3. Finally, you will put on a silent skit, showing these persons to the class.
4. The class will then discuss the characteristics you allowed your person to display.

SAMPLE CHARACTER STUDIES:

1. She was young and tall, very tall, but she was hunched over as if she were an old woman. Her long blond hair hung in stringy bangs over her eyes and down to the middle of her back. Her clothes were baggy and unflattering. As I came near her, I saw the smudges of dirt on her cheeks, or perhaps they were bruises. I followed her as she came to the school. She walked quickly, with long strides, head bent down, as she passed the rowdy crowd...

2. He was handsome, tall, muscular, confident. He walked with his head high in the air and shoved any who stood in his way as he passed down the hall of the school. He glanced at those less fortunate than he with an air of disgust and pushed those who stood in front of his locker into the crowd...

NCTE Standard for Language Arts: Students use spoken, written, and visual language to accomplish their own purposes (e.g., for learning, enjoyment, persuasion, and the exchange of information).

DESCRIBING CHARACTERS FROM AN EXTERIOR VIEWPOINT

ASSIGNMENTS AND GUIDELINES:

This week, you will be designing characters. You will describe them from an exterior viewpoint, from a place as if you were standing near them. As you write, be sure to begin at one place on the character's figure and move slowly out from that point. Your success will depend upon the DETAIL that you incorporate in your description. Here is a list of your assignments for the week:

1. You will design five characters in writing.
2. The characters you choose to describe can be of any age, any size, and any sex. They need not be human.
3. The character you choose to describe may be from any time period: past, present, or future.
4. Be sure to include skin and clothing texture, colors, or smells (as if you are right next to this person).
5. Finally, after you complete your paragraphs, choose the character you like the best, and memorize the paragraph describing this person. If possible, get a costume and props (if needed), and present your character to the class.
6. If time permits, you could critique each other's creations.

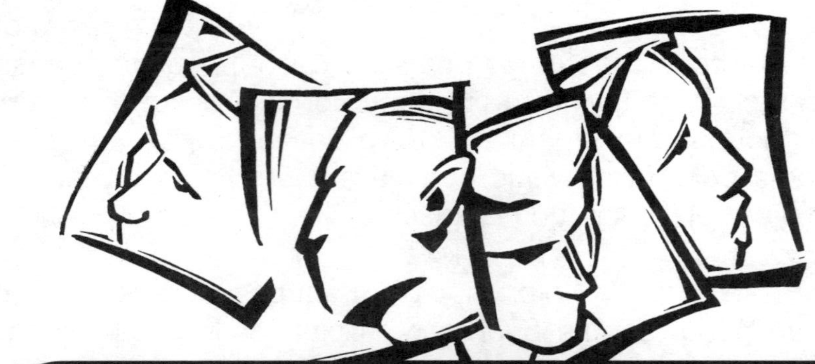

SUGGESTIONS AND IDEAS:

1. I believe he said his name was John Henry Woodson, III. As I came up behind him, I noticed the polished shine on the top of his head. Small, fine, white flakes of skin mingled with what little hair he had, which was combed down as if pointing to the floor. He reached back when he realized I stood behind him and took a cup of tea from the tray I held. His face was tanned and smooth—the face of the non-working class. He had white, perfectly kept teeth, a straight nose, and no unwanted facial hair showing. He had a very thin neck with a bobbing Adam's apple. His voice was deep and soft. Perfectly spoken syllables, clipped sentences. He was sitting down in a wingback chair. Knees crossed. Confident and comfortable in these luxurious surroundings...

2. Mrs. Mable Gray entered the office on a Saturday morning. It was snowing heavily, and she carried a huge blue umbrella, from which she shook the snow all over the office floor. The umbrella contrasted nicely with the voluminous, bright orange-red hair that was pinned atop her head. Her face was rosy and scrubbed. Well-used laugh lines bracketed her eyes and lips. A white ruffled blouse circled her neck, and fur surrounded the ruffles. Her coat was tattered and even torn in one spot. A long, black skirt hung beneath the uneven hem of the coat, and a white, ragged, ruffled petticoat beneath that...

NCTE Language Arts Standard: Students use spoken, written, and visual language to accomplish their own purposes (e.g., for learning, enjoyment, persuasion, and the exchange of information).

DESIGNING CHARACTERS

ASSIGNMENTS AND GUIDELINES:

This week you will be writing about different kinds of characters. To begin, you will use the first day to think about all kinds of characters. You will do this by making an organized list. This is one way to make your list:

Type of Character:	Brief Description:	Personality:
1. A Tyrannosaurus rex that's a vegetarian. name: Smudge	This dinosaur has a very sad look on his face all the time. He wears a green floppy hat in honor of the vegetables he loves. He also lives alone because none of the other dinosaurs want to play with him.	Smudge is a warm-hearted fellow. In fact, one day as he's romping through the forest, he finds a sick little bunny that appears to be abandoned by its family. Smudge gently picks it up and brings it home to care for it in his cave.
2. A robot that was made at a big robot plant and then thrown into the trash heap outside of a small town in South Dakota in the middle of winter	The robot is big, about the size of a grown person. It is all dented and wires are sticking out of its belly in all directions. Its eyes are bright-red glass reflectors. After two days in the pile of trash and deep snow, the eyes start blinking ... then, they steadily light up.	The robot has a brilliant personality, but has a deep, dark secret. He has FEELINGS! This is something robots must NOT have, and he feels like a failure and is very ashamed.

After making a list of characters, it is time to write a story about some or all of the characters, retelling characteristics about each in narrative form. Your assignment for the rest of the week is to write at least one story (you may write several), telling about the characters you have designed. When you have completed all the designs, you may choose your favorite character and illustrate him/her on a piece of art paper.

STORY EXAMPLES:

My first character is a robot that has been discarded by the National Robot Institute because he has not lived up to expectations. The robots produced by this institute are in charge of examining and testing the electrical circuits of missiles. When the robot was placed at his quality control station, all he could think about were all the people who would be endangered by these missiles. So, he decided to play sick. He fell down on the floor and clanked his arms and legs all over the place until they came and carried him away to the repair lab. After a time, they saw that he was unable to do his job, so they tore him apart and discarded him in a dump one snowy day in December.

My second character is the little girl named Wanda who FINDS the above-mentioned robot and drags him home on her new electronically controlled sled that she received for her birthday. Wanda lives with her Aunt Gertrude in a drafty old house ten miles from the robot-producing factory. Wanda sneaks the robot up to her bedroom where she immediately begins working on him with the new electronic analysis kit she also got for her birthday. Did I happen to mention, she's a genius?

NCTE Standard for Language Arts: Students use spoken, written, and visual language to accomplish their own purposes (e.g., for learning, enjoyment, persuasion, and the exchange of information).

DESIGNING SETTINGS

ASSIGNMENTS AND GUIDELINES:

This week, you will be writing various settings. According to *Webster's Unabridged Dictionary*, "setting," in writing, is defined thus: **Setting** - time and place, environment, background, or surroundings. Actual physical surroundings or scenery, whether real, as a garden, or artificial, as on a stage.

Keeping this definition in mind, you are to complete the following assignments this week.

1. The first step to writing a setting is to brainstorm and make lists of various aspects of a setting. Take about fifteen minutes and make a list similar to the following:

	TIME:	PLACE:	ENVIRONMENT:
a.	late at night →	in a haunted house in Ohio →	dark, damp, creepy, and old
b.	in the future, 2020 →	at Cape Canaveral →	heading for Mars
c	in 1620, the Colonies →	stepping off the *Mayflower* →	cold, forested, rocky beach
d.	present day →	waking up high in a tree →	flat plains covered with snow
e.	evening →	deserted street in New York →	foggy, rainy, and cool
f.	early morning →	at home, in your bed →	the house is empty

2. After brainstorming your list, choose the ideas you want to develop, and write four settings (each one must be set in a different place and time).
3. After you have written your four first drafts, choose the one that is your favorite, then edit and revise the draft completely. If time remains, have a friend edit the draft and have him/her make suggestions.
4. Make your final draft either in your best handwriting or on the computer, if one is available.
5. After your final draft has been completed, glue the paper on a piece of white or colored tagboard. In one of the corners, draw and color an illustration of your setting. A sample layout is on the right.
6. Be prepared to share your setting at the appropriate time.

SUGGESTIONS AND LAYOUT:

Here is a setting excerpt that may help you see the detail necessary when designing a setting:

She was reading by candle-light, the night that the storm came. It began as a low, howling wind and grew to a roar. She had been sitting in a soft chair before the fire and had covered herself with a quilt. A steaming cup of tea sat next to her on the table. The rain and hail smashed against the windows and walls of the house. Suddenly, there was a loud crash! She ran to the kitchen where the door had blown open, shattering the panes across the floor. A sound like an approaching train filled the rooms. The floor began to tremble, the china fell one by one from the shelves. She ran to the window and strained to see through the torrent. Then, in terror, she retreated, running and tripping down into the basement. She lay under the staircase and covered herself with the old quilt. The sound was unbearable! Then it was silent, just as quickly as it came ... it left. When she uncovered herself, she looked up and saw the stars...

Title of Setting	ILLUSTRATION CAN BE PLACED HERE
SETTING GOES HERE	SETTING (cont.

NCTE Standard for Language Arts: Students employ a wide range of strategies as they write and use different writing process elements appropriately to communicate with different audiences for a variety of purposes.

Dr. Jekyll and Mr. Hyde

ASSIGNMENTS AND GUIDELINES:

This week, you will work alone to write diary entries that are written by Dr. Jekyll and Mr. Hyde. As you know, the man had two opposing personalities. You will pretend to be each "person." Dr. Jekyll made a potion that caused him to develop another personality. Dr. Jekyll became the madman, Mr. Hyde, after drinking the potion. Mr. Hyde is a sinister, evil person, while Dr. Jekyll is kind and gentle. Each time Jekyll took a dose of the potion, he became Mr. Hyde. He had severe reactions to it and did horrible things. You will pretend to be BOTH of these characters and to write of your experiences in a diary. Here are the assignments for the week:

1. You will prepare a small booklet that will serve as a diary. It should look old and worn. A cloth cover would look authentic.
2. You will write daily entries, and you may alternate in whatever way you wish, but one day you will be Jekyll, and another day you will be Hyde.
3. After writing at least ten entries, memorize two of your entries and perform the persons of Jekyll and Hyde for the class.

IDEAS FOR DIARY ENTRIES:

1. **January 10, 1885** – I am in the laboratory. It is night. I am intrigued with a new substance I have worked on for the past few months, and it is in the final stages. I have a pair of white rats that I have kept for the injection. I pick up one of the animals. It squirms in my hand as I insert the needle. The candlelight flickers suddenly from an unexpected movement of air. I wonder about this, for the windows are tightly shut. The animal jerks and bites me as I return it to his cage. It runs around frantically, and unexpectedly attacks the other mouse in the cage, biting it on its neck.

2. **January 15, 1885** – I am released from that absolutely useless Jekyll. It is midnight now, and earlier, I walked into the streets of London to see what I could find. I have longed to have the golden cane in old Mr. Wigginton's shop. I took a large rock and smashed the front window. I have the handmade cane in my hand now. What a beautiful creation!

NCTE Standard for Language Arts: Students adjust their use of spoken, written, and visual language (e.g., conventions, style, vocabulary) to communicate effectively with a variety of audiences and for different purposes.

EDITING YOUR WRITING

HOW TO EDIT:

Editing is one of the most important things that authors do when they write something. **Editing** is the process of correcting mistakes you make when you write. When you write any piece, it is a good idea to skip spaces on the paper to leave room for editing. It is also a good idea to write your piece at least two times before doing a final copy. When you rewrite a piece of writing, you usually want to change a lot of ideas. That is called "REVISING." AFTER you revise your writing, it is probably a good idea to edit the work one more time.

On the right side of this page is a sample of an **UNEDITED** piece. Now it needs to be **EDITED**. Here is a list of the things you correct when you edit your work. The symbols below are the symbols that you write on your first draft to indicate it needs to be changed. You should also use a colored pen to edit, so when you do the next draft, you will be alerted to things you must change.

1. **Spelling errors**
2. **Capitalization errors**
3. **Punctuation errors**
4. **Paragraphing errors**
5. **Grammatical errors**
6. **Too many words**
7. **Skipped word or words**
8. **Wrong word errors**

- (sp) **> used to show a possible incorrectly spelled word**
- **> used to show that a word or words need to be removed**
- ¶ **> used when you must indent for a new paragraph**
- ^ **> used to insert a letter, phrase, sentence, or punctuation**
- / **> used to change a capital to a lowercase letter**
- ≡ **> used to change a lowercase letter to a capital**
- ⊙ **> used to show the need for a period**
- ^, **> used to show the need for a comma**
- ^" ^" **> used to show the need for quotation marks**

EDITING A SAMPLE:

Correct all the mistakes in the following sample paragraph. Use the symbols on the bottom left of this page. Do the correction right on this sheet, preferably in a colored pen. Remember, you are only looking for capitalization, punctuation, spelling, left out words, too many words, and so on. When you complete the sheet, discuss the corrections you made with a partner, and then hand the sheet to your teacher.

Once upun a tim ina land far away ther was a big ugly dragon who lived in a cave he was a veri lonly dragont becuse everyone ran away from him becuse they thot he wood eat them up in a big big big gulp The dragon desided he wood show the people of the village that he was nice one day at dawn he he picked an enormous bunch of sunflowers then he went to each hause and nocked at the door ever so gently and layed a sunflower at the feet of the owner.

NCTE Standard for Language Arts: Students employ a wide range of strategies as they write and use different writing process elements appropriately to communicate with different audiences for a variety of purposes.

EXTERNAL CONFLICT

ASSIGNMENTS AND GUIDELINES:

This week, you will work with a partner to develop a skit that depicts external conflict. It may be advisable that you read a few selections that characterize this element before you begin. The following is a list of your assignments for this week:

1. You will first develop an idea for a conflicting situation. One idea is given on the right. An external conflict comes from **outside** yourself. Some types of EXTERNAL CONFLICTS are:
   a. **PERSONAL CONFLICT:** This would be a conflict with another person or persons. Example story: The relationship between Scrooge and everyone else in *A Christmas Carol.*
   b. **ENVIRONMENTAL CONFLICT:** This would be a conflict with the weather or the land. Example story: *The Call of the Wild.*
   c. **SITUATIONAL CONFLICT:** This would be a conflict where the character(s) find themslves in a bad situation, like financial troubles or loss of a job. Example story: *Oliver Twist* or *David Copperfield.*
2. With your partner, you will take your idea and write a short play or skit that clearly shows one or more of these types of conflict.
3. You and your partner will then perfect this play by acting it out and seeing how the events flow.
4. Write or type on the computer the edited and revised play.
5. Memorize your parts and present the play before the class.
6. As you watch each partnership present its play, try to identify the conflict each group is portraying. Discuss these. See if you can identify the category into which each situation fits.
7. Perhaps the class can discuss how both of you handled the problem.

A SAMPLE SCRIPT OF AN ENVIRONMENTAL CONFLICT:

SARA: Paula, did you hear the forecast? There's a possibility of severe weather coming into the mountains tonight. Can you imagine ... in April? Just our luck, the first real vacation we've had in years, and now we'll be stranded. I swear, we live under a dark cloud.

PAULA: Well, we could leave right now, but we'll lose the deposit on the cabin. Dad said we were nuts to come here. Uh-oh, look outside! The snow has already started. How about food, did we bring enough? Chuck said the basement is well stocked. There's a pantry down there. Let's go look. There's a huge stack of firewood out back. I saw it when I checked to see if the basement door was locked. We can bring in wood as we need it. (Paula and Sara go down to the basement.)

SARA: The supplies look ample. There must be a hundred cans of food down here. And look here, there's a large can of oil for the lanterns and lamps. Flashlights, candles, and here is a rifle, unloaded. We might end up having to shoot a bear or something. (They laugh.)

PAULA: What was that? Did you hear that? It sounded like a thump coming from upstairs. There, there it is again. Did you hear it? Did you bolt the front door?...

NCTE Standard for Language Arts: Students use a variety of technological and information resources (e.g., libraries, databases, computer networks, videos, maps) to gather and synthesize information and to create and communicate knowledge.

FOLKTALE RETELLING

ASSIGNMENTS AND GUIDELINES:

This week, you will be writing folktales. To refresh your memory, **folktales** are stories that were not written down but were told from one generation to the next. They probably ended up being far from any truth, if that is indeed what they were based upon. These tales usually originated in particular cultures, and for that reason, we have folktales from Sweden, from Poland, from Africa, and every other country in the world. These stories have historic events sprinkled within them. Many times, they have a lesson or moral in them like fables. One of the Internet dictionaries gives two different definitions of the word "folktale":

1. A folktale is a story or legend forming part of an oral tradition.

2. A folktale is a tale circulated by word of mouth among the common folk.

Your assignment therefore is to complete the following:

1. You are to do research in the school library on folktales. If possible, find folktales that relate to your own ancestry or choose another.
2. Choose one folktale that you have read and rewrite the story in your own words. Tell it as if you are a storyteller and you have heard this story from a poor peasant in the last village that you visited.
3. If you would rather make up your own folktale, perhaps you can use some of the story starter sentences in the box at the right.
4. After you have written your tale, memorize it, obtain a costume of either a storyteller or a traveling vagabond or just a poor peasant from another time, and tell the story for the class. Perhaps your performances could be videotaped.
5. Finally, discuss the storytelling you saw, and evaluate the stories. Discuss how authentic each one sounded. Make kindly suggestions.

STORY STARTERS:

1. *It was a dreary, dark, and stormy night...*
2. *There once was a young boy who often told lies...*
3. *There once lived three sisters who were looking for husbands...*
4. *One day, a young girl was hoeing her mother's garden when she saw something glistening...*
5. *Two women were on a train going to a far country...*
6. *A man had two women whom he loved, but he did not know how to choose which one to marry, so he decided...*
7. *There was once a king who had three conniving sons. He had to choose one to rule his kingdom, so he consulted a wise old man whom he knew...*
8. *Long ago, there were no animals roaming the wild west. So one wise old man, who had many hungry children in his family, decided to go to a person who was known to perform magical feats...*

NCTE Standard for Language Arts: Students use spoken, written, and visual language to accomplish their own purposes (e.g., for learning, enjoyment, persuasion, and the exchange of information).

Ghost Story

ASSIGNMENTS & GUIDELINES:

This week, you will be working alone to write a ghost story. You may not believe in ghosts, but you may find it fun to think about and write in this exciting storytelling style. You will have about one week to complete the following assignments:

1. You will write a ghost story using some of the ideas listed to the right or from your own ideas.
2. After you complete your first draft, share it with your cooperative group. One person in the group should be assigned as the secretary to take notes. The group may give you ideas or suggestions for your story. You do not have to accept their suggestions, or you may want to incorporate a few of the suggestions into your final story.
3. Edit your first draft, rewrite it, and either type it or write it very neatly, with changes, into a final draft.
4. Draw and paint a picture of your ghost or the house or place where your ghost lived.
5. Be ready to share a short summary of your story and your painting next week sometime!

ONE IDEA FOR A STORY LINE:

Your mom or dad has suddenly received word that they have to move to a snowy northern state. When you move and get settled into your new (old) home, you find out that:

1. The house you have moved into was built in 1889 by a carpenter for his new wife, who died suddenly while giving birth to their first child.
2. The man was sent into a deep wave of depression, and his sister came and took the new baby to her home and raised it along with her own son.
3. The distraught husband died suddenly a few months later after he fell from a ladder leading to the attic.
4. The attic was sealed off, never to be opened again, until your family moves into the house, over one hundred years later. Your dad breaks the seals leading to the attic.
5. A few weeks after you move in, you are awakened one night by the sound of a pounding in the attic. The attic door is in your own bedroom, so you go to tell your parents, and they tell you to sleep in the guest room...

NCTE Standard for Language Arts: Students employ a wide range of strategies as they write and use different writing process elements appropriately to communicate with different audiences for a variety of purposes.

THE GRASS IS ALWAYS GREENER...

ASSIGNMENTS AND GUIDELINES:

This week, you will write about a person who is dissatisfied with his/her present state of life, no matter <u>how</u> good his/her life is. As you write, try to remember the times when you thought that someone's life looked better than yours. You perhaps thought that if your life was like theirs, then you could be happy. Here are your guidelines for writing this week:

1. The first thing you will do is design three characters who are dissatisfied with the way their lives are going. Some things you may want to tell about each are where this person lives, what he/she looks like, what kind of possessions he/she has, who his/her friends are, what kind of work he/she does, and so on.
2. After you have designed all your characters, choose the best character that you have, and develop a news story about this person and the opportunity that arises that enables him/her to change his/her life entirely. Perhaps he/she finds a secret coin with which he/she can make three wishes. Perhaps he/she wins the lottery or a rich uncle leaves him/her a huge estate. Perhaps he/she magically changes places with someone.
3. Write the story about your person and his/her seemingly good luck.
4. Finally, write a news report about the person. Include his/her previous situation, and then tell about the turn of events. When you have completed the report, perform your report as though you were a news reporter.
5. If you have access to a video camera, you may want to do a video story of this person like they do on some television news shows. For example, when they do reports on the life of a special person or the life of a person who had something extraordinary happen to him/her. Incorporate the news report into the video.

SUGGESTED STORYLINES:

1. Walter Samuels, III, woke when he heard a light tap upon his bedroom door. It was the servant with breakfast. Oh bother! Why did he ALWAYS have to "eat a good breakfast"? Walter's one wish was that, someday, he would be free of all this fussiness—the house that teemed with servants, the nanny who insisted that he study at least four hours a day, the miles and miles of property he could never investigate if he tried from now till doomsday...
2. Carlotta looked at herself in the long mirror. She was short and thin (some would say skinny). Instead of looking like a senior in high school, she looked like an eighth grader! Her hair was long and limp, the color of mud. She was shy and had never been out on a date. Besides that, her dad wouldn't even let her go to a football game with her best friend Laura. Her clothes were all secondhand, and all she ever did was take care of her five brothers and sisters. If only something would save her from this wretched misery...
3. Molly lifted the tiny baby from the crib and held it to her chest. If only Ted would be able to find a job today. The baby needed milk, and the rent was overdue. They had no food to eat in the house. She sat down on the sofa and placed her face in her hands. She placed the baby beside her and reached for the newspaper want ads. Maybe SHE could find a job, and Ted could stay home with the baby...

NCTE Standard for Language Arts: Students participate as knowledgeable, reflective, creative, and critical members of a variety of literacy communities.

INTERNAL CONFLICT

ASSIGNMENTS AND GUIDELINES:

This week, you will be working alone to complete the following tasks:

1. You will read the definition of internal conflict as stated in the box at the right. Then you will read the samples of internal conflict shown to the right, also.
2. You will write a first draft of a selection showing a character suffering from this situation.
3. Within your draft, your character must face situations that cause him/her frustration, distress, or difficulty.
4. When you complete the draft, edit and revise as often as necessary. Then complete the final draft, preferably typed.
5. On the art paper your teacher provides, portray, with an illustration, internal conflict. You may have several illustrations to accompany your writing, if you wish.

DEFINITION OF INTERNAL: inward, from within; of or on the inside.
DEFINITION OF CONFLICT: a fight; battle; struggle; emotional disturbance resulting from a clash of impulses in a person.
from SIMON and SCHUSTER'S, *WEBSTER'S NEW TWENTIETH CENTURY DICTIONARY OF THE ENGLISH LANGUAGE*

EXAMPLES OF INTERNAL CONFLICT:

1. Internal conflict would exist in the case of a child like Pinocchio who always wanted to be a real boy but was really a wooden boy.
2. Internal conflict would also exist in the case of a teenager who continually wants to be accepted by a certain group of people who want nothing to do with him/her.
3. It would exist in the case of a student who wanted to maintain a degree of excellence that would be humanly impossible. This situation could be in academic areas, athletics, or as a daughter or son trying to live up to an expectation set by parents or himself/herself.
4. It would be prevalent in the case of a child who tells his/her parents that he/she knows someone or something is living in their attic, but they will not believe him/her.
5. There was internal conflict in Cinderella's life as she was constantly abused by her stepsisters and stepmother.
6. Conflict would be in a child who is bullied by an older student on the school bus.

NCTE Standard for Language Arts: Students adjust their use of spoken, written, and visual language (like conventions, style, vocabulary), to communicate effectively with a variety of audiences and for different purposes.

Klutz finds Klutz

ASSIGNMENTS AND GUIDELINES:

This week, you will be writing a story in the first person. You will pretend to be the friend of a very klutzy person (either a girl or boy), and you will somehow work out a way to have your friend meet the person he or she is destined to meet. One way to do this is to have your friend place an ad in the personal column of the newspaper. Another idea is to fix him or her up on a blind date. Whatever your method, write a story about your plan, the way it came about, and the result. When you complete your story, place it on a poster, with pictures of the klutz and klutzee for all to see. You may either draw and color the illustrations, or you may have two of your friends pose for them and take photographs.

KLUTZ **KLUTZEE**

SAMPLE SELECTION:

Well, I really don't know where to start, it's all so weird and all, but here goes. It all started one snowy day when we stayed home from school. My best friend just happens to be a total geek. Well, he's not exactly a geek, more like a nerd, well, not that either, exactly, anyway he's a genuine and I mean, GENUINE, klutz. You just wouldn't believe it. It's not <u>one</u> day we get on the bus, not ONCE, mind you, that he doesn't trip on the steps and hit his head on the steering wheel. You see, he's also very tall. My mom says his feet are so far from his brain that they just can't get their act together.

Anyway, on the day it snowed, I got on my boots and jacket and trudged over to Freddy's (my klutzy friend's). He was down in the family room, playing on his computer. (Did I happen to mention Freddy is a computer genius?) Anyway, his mom brought down some hot chocolate, and we were sitting there just chewing the fat, when out of the clear blue, Freddy asks me if I would consider him a good-looking guy. As he put it, "You know, a guy a girl could fall for?" I couldn't resist and answered that I didn't know if a girl could exactly fall for him, but I knew that he could definitely fall for her! He didn't laugh, and then I knew he was serious. I told him that he wasn't BAD-looking, but he sure wasn't any Tom Cruise. He asked me if I had a date for the prom yet, and I said I was taking Marsha Berkowitz, which he already knew. Then he dropped the big one. He asked me if I would help him find a date for the prom.

Well, I knew right then, we had a MAJOR job on our hands! But, after some thought, an idea started rolling around in this old brain...

NCTE Standard for Language Arts: Students adjust their use of spoken, written, and visual language (e.g., conventions, style, vocabulary) to communicate effectively with a variety of audiences and for different purposes.

KNIGHT SAVES DAMSEL IN DISTRESS

ASSIGNMENTS AND GUIDELINES:

This week, you will be writing a newspaper article for a newspaper in the Middle Ages. Actually, they probably had no real newspapers, but they may have had something like a handwritten newsletter that was rolled up scroll fashion and read aloud by a courier who traveled from one manor to another, announcing the local news and gossip. The "knight in shining armor" image was really quite true. The knights were very brave soldiers, and upon being knighted, they swore to defend not only their lord (who was the landowner who had supported them through knight training) but also the Church and all those in need of help (which at that time included women). Your duty this week is to write a report on one of these daring rescues of a young maiden by a courageous knight. When you finish your story, obtain a long piece of paper, and write your story in your best longhand or calligraphy, if you know how to write in this manner. This paper will serve as your scroll. On the assigned day, you will read your account for the class. Be sure to write your story in the finest King's English, noble and true, like knighthood itself.

SAMPLE STORY EXCERPT:

Hear Ye, Hear Ye, all friends of the Lord and Lady Wendal who abide in the west of Scotland. A feast will be held ten days hence from the morrow, on the thirtieth of October, in the year of our Lord, one thousand fifteen. All having good wishes are invited to this feast to celebrate the magnificent and heroic deed done by the young sir Gerard, just one and twenty years of age. He smote the terrible villain, Viscoat, stabbing him thrice through the heart. He devised a great and very dangerous plan when he saw that the villain had captured and bound the hands and feet of the young maiden, Clare Wendal. It is truly a tragic tale...

NCTE Standard for Language Arts: Students employ a wide range of strategies as they write and use different writing process elements appropriately to communicate with different audiences for a variety of purposes.

LEGENDS

ASSIGNMENTS AND GUIDELINES:

This week, you will be writing a skit that portrays a legendary character. Legends are stories about people who are good and SO real in the story that it is hard to believe that they may not be true. Legends are written about very great, strong, powerful persons that may or may not have existed. Some great legendary figures are Davy Crockett, King Arthur, Calamity Jane, Wyatt Earp, Doc Holliday, and Robin Hood. The characteristics of a legend are as follows:

1. They contain a hero who is himself or herself a "legend."
2. The hero or heroine does powerful things for the good of mankind.
3. The stories about this person have the following characters in them: usually the hero, a villain, a victim, and a partner or friend.
4. The stories have a plot or problem and a solution to that problem.

After doing some research about legendary characters, your assignment is to write a skit involving a legendary character.

Definition of the word **legend:** a story of some wonderful event, handed down for generations and believed to have some historical basis, but is not verifiable

SAMPLE DIALOGUE:

The following script segment is from a story about King Arthur and one of his young squires, Boyyent, who has just offered to represent Camelot, Arthur's castle, in the upcoming joust. Arthur is hesitant to send this young man into the joust, for some of the knights are aggressive, and he does not wish Boyyent to go against them. Arthur has always thought of this boy as a son and is protective of him:

<u>Squire Boyyent</u>: *Sire, I would like very much to be in the joust, for, as you know, I am a somewhat successful bowman and I am sure I could bring honor to your name.*

<u>King Arthur</u>: *Boyyent, my dear boy, I know, without a doubt, that you bring nothing but honor to our name, but it is a matter of experience. You are too young and have not the experience necessary for the event. Therefore, I would like you to accompany Sir Lancelot and Sir Wallfort to the games and help them in their preparations. But, I do <u>not</u> want you to act as a participant, not at this time. Perhaps at the next event.*

<u>Squire Boyyent</u>: *Yes...Yes...but Sire, I wish very passionately to participate.*

<u>King Arthur</u>: *That is my final decision.*

NCTE Standard for Language Arts: Students adjust their use of spoken, written, and visual language (e.g., conventions, style, vocabulary) to communicate effectively with a variety of audiences and for different purposes.

Magical Hat

ASSIGNMENTS AND GUIDELINES:

This week you will be writing details, details, details. You will write all the things you see when you find a magical hat. The following lists your assignments for the week:

1. You will be working with a partner or in a small group to design four magical hats, each of which has special powers.
2. Each member will then go off by himself/herself to write a little story about each of the hats. Each student will write four short stories, each involving one of the four hats.
3. After you have done the writing, you will come back with your partner or group and share your stories with the group. Discuss changes, additions, or deletions needed for each selection, then rewrite them in final form. If you have the opportunity, type the selections on the computer.
4. You will then come back with the group and illustrate all four of the hats on large art paper.
5. Finally, your group will do an oral presentation of your hat illustrations and as many of the hat "stories" as you have time to share.
6. If it is possible, videotape your presentations.

IDEAS FOR MAGICAL HATS:

1. You could find an old battered top hat that gives off sparks when you find it. It is a dusty, muddied silk hat with its lid torn and hanging from it. When you place it on your head, it transports you to another world or planet that is populated by tiny persons.
2. You are spelunking in a dark cave one summer day, and you find a huge hobo hat that sits atop a growing stalagmite. You turn it over and set it upside down on the floor of the cave. Suddenly, the hat begins spewing toys and stuffed animals that are alive!
3. You are in a hat shop in a quaint part of town and lift a large, wide-brimmed, feathered Victorian hat from the shelf. It leaps upon your head and lifts you from the ground! You fly from the store and rise into the air above the ground. You find yourself in a magical kingdom in the clouds. The dazzling queen of the kingdom bows to you.

NCTE Standard for Language Arts: Students employ a wide range of strategies as they write and use different writing process elements appropriately to communicate with different audiences for a variety of purposes.

Making a Classroom Newspaper

ASSIGNMENTS AND GUIDELINES:

This week, you will be writing articles for a group newspaper. You will be working with a group to do this, and your teacher will approve the material you will gather. Some suggestions for articles are listed below. Here are your assignments for the week:

1. You can choose about four to six articles to write in your newspaper from the list below. If you have another idea for an article, check with your teacher to see if it is permissible.
2. After you have written the articles, type them on the computer, or print them neatly on paper. Glue or tape each article on a large sheet as shown at the right. Think of a good name for your paper.
   a. You can interview your principal and ask her about her job—how she likes it, the hard and easy parts of the work, etc.
   b. You can report on the school football team or another team in your school or a local sports group.
   c. You can interview a student in the school who recently came from another part of the U.S. or another country.
   d. You may write about a long-term assignment that you have and give the class some ideas about how to complete the assignment in your article.
   e. You may report on an upcoming schoolwide event and list the preparations or help that is needed for this event.
   f. You can report on a local event in your area that families may want to attend, like the county fair.

FRONT SIDE OF PAPER

MR. PENN'S PALS

SOCCER NEWS

Mr. Penn's class polished off Mrs. Murphy's class in the spring soccer game. It was a heart-stopping, action-packed game! Congratulations to both teams for a game well played!

PRINCIPALS HAVE ONE TOUGH JOB!

Principal Brown has more work than any of us would ever know. Not only does he have to keep the whole school running smoothly, but he also has to fill out mounds and mounds of paperwork. Thanks to you for all you do, Mr. Brown!!

WHAT'S COMING UP IN OUR SCHOOL

The science fair is quickly approaching! Get your posters ready for display. Remember to complete your registration form by next Friday and get it into Miss Sampas's mailbox in the school office.

EARTH DAY!!

Make sure that you and your family plan to come to Earth Day at the Greenfield Community Park this Saturday. There will be lots of fun activities and food. Everyone will get a free tree to plant!

BACK SIDE OF PAPER

Student of the Week

NEW STUDENT FROM FRANCE

Welcome to Pierre Lamond! He has just moved here from France. He said he loves America! He said that he does miss the rest of his family who are still in his country, but his family plans on visiting him every summer.

MRS. RIPLEY HAS A SCARY VACATION, YIKES!

Mrs. Ripley got a big surprise when she visited Yosemite National Park last summer. She was setting up her tent on the grounds when all of a sudden...

NCTE Standard for Language Arts: Students use a variety of technological and information resources (e.g., libraries, databases, computer networks, videos, or maps) to gather and synthesize information and to create and communicate knowledge.

MAPPING YOUR FANTASY

ASSIGNMENTS AND GUIDELINES:

This week, you will be designing a large map on the paper your teacher provides for you. Your assignments are as follows:

1. You will think of a place of which you would like to make a map. It may be a place in a book that you are reading or a place in your dreams or imagination. There are some ideas for places you might use listed at the right.
2. When you have an idea, you will first draw it out in rough form, in pencil, on loose-leaf paper. You may have to make several rough drafts before you have what you want.
3. Design a **MAP KEY** for your map like the keys at the bottom of your classroom maps or the maps in your books. You may show a variety of things using symbols of your choice.
4. You could show mountains and valleys with a textured surface, like stripes, polka-dots, checks, or plaids, and lakes with another pattern. Be as creative as you can.
5. Draw and name all the buildings, landmarks, schools, and parks in the area.
6. When you have completed your design, transfer it to the good paper, drawing it first in pencil. Then color it with markers or crayons.
7. Prepare to share your map with the class.

SUGGESTIONS FOR MAPS:

1. You could make a map of a peppermint candy factory, an ice cream factory, a cake-baking plant, a doughnut shop, or a chocolate city with milkshake rivers.
2. You could make a map of a village with houses made of gingerbread or peppermint sticks with chocolate wafers for the roof tiles.
3. You could make a map of a village on another planet, with aliens in the streets. The streets could be in the air. Mountains could be a volcano range. Buildings could be ultra-modern with alien names. Rivers could be frozen, or maybe even glaciers. Everyone could live in a huge bubble.
4. You could make a map of a village that is upside down. The houses and mountains and streets are in the sky and face the ground. The people walk upside down, held in place by weird gravity fields. Have FUN!

NCTE Standard for Language Arts: Students employ a wide range of strategies as they write and use different writing process elements appropriately to communicate with different audiences for a variety of purposes.

ONOMATOPOEIA

ASSIGNMENTS AND GUIDELINES:

Have you ever gone to the automobile repair shop and heard one of your parents say, "Well, when the car first starts up, it goes ping, ping, ping, chug, chug, chug, and clunk."

Well, what your parent is trying to make is a reproduction of the sound that your car makes. That use of language is called **onomatopoeia**. It is a lot of fun to write with this type of language. Your assignment is as follows:

1. You will brainstorm with your cooperative learning group to come up with as many onomatopoeic words as you can. This will serve as your word bank when you begin part two.
2. You will do the assignment alone from this point. You will pretend that you are employed as a writer/artist for a large New York advertising firm. You have been asked to write the text, design, and illustrate a brochure that advertises a new ride at a theme park, a new toy produced by a large company, or any item that you think will lend itself to onomatopoeic language.
3. First, you should write your text. Be sure to edit and revise it well before you place it on the good brochure paper. You may want to type your article on the computer. Print it out, and then cut and paste the paragraphs onto the brochure paper.
4. Be sure to place a colorful illustration on the front of the brochure to make your item tempting.

SAMPLE BROCHURE TEXT:

SWOOSH, SLIDE, SWOOSH, SLIDE, SWOOSH, SWASH, SWASH!! This is the sound of the newest, most exciting ride (if you can call it that) at the "Peter Piper Plenty-of-Playfulness Theme Park." On this ride, "The Chamber," you will experience the "can't-catch-your-breath syndrome" and feel the THUMP, THUMP of your heart as it tries to leap from your chest. You will hear the wind whip past your ears, WHOOSH, and press against your chest! It is one of the most thrilling rides of the century. It begins as you are placed into a chamber with one other person. As you are strapped in at your chest and ankles, you hear the far off roar of an engine, and the sound becomes closer and closer until you realize...

NCTE Standard for Language Arts: Students adjust their use of spoken, written, and visual language (e.g., conventions, style, vocabulary) to communicate effectively with a variety of audiences and for different purposes.

PIZZAZZY PARTS OF SPEECH

ASSIGNMENTS AND GUIDELINES:

This week, you will be working in a group of three or four persons to develop lists of words. You will write each type of word on a piece of chart paper. Here are the assignments for the week:

1. You will get six strips of chart paper that will be provided by your teacher.
2. At the top of each strip, you will write these headings:
   1st strip: **NOUNS** 4th strip: **ARTICLES**
   2nd strip: **VERBS** 5th strip: **ADJECTIVES**
   3rd strip: **PREPOSITIONS** 6th strip: **NOUNS**
3. You will then work together to list, in broad-tipped marker, as many words as you can of each part of speech on the paper labeled with that name. (A sample is given on the right.)
4. After you have listed these words, your group will be sharing the lists with the class. It is important that you hang the lists on the board or wall for all the class to see in the order listed above.
5. You will call upon the members of the class to make up crazy sentences using your word lists. All they have to do is pick one word from each column to make a sentence. (They might have to add a word here and there.)
6. After all the class has shared their lists and left them hanging, you will use these wonderful lists to write a **MAGICAL STORY.** Don't be afraid to mix things together that do not usually go together. It can be fun to use your pencil as a paintbrush!

NOUNS	VERBS	PREPOSITIONS	ARTICLES	ADJECTIVES	NOUNS
Ernie	flew	over	the	slimy	sludge
mice	wiggled	under	an	fluffy	pile
house	smashed	through	a	icy	bank
food	walked	around		slippery	kitchen
buildings	dripped	down		crunchy	street
airplanes	soared	beneath		beastly	caverns
New York	melted	beyond		empty	frying pans
apples	jumped	from		sparkling	snowflakes
etc.	etc.	etc.		etc.	etc.

Once upon a wintery night, a small willowy wren named Willie was seen hopping over piles of crunchy, grape-colored, snow-covered leaves. Suddenly, something caught his eye. He could barely make out the enormous shape as it stomped down the snow-blanketed path toward him. Then he realized, when he saw the long swinging trunk coming nearer, it was Herman, the bald, blue elephant! His old buddy! Herman almost crushed the wren under his monstrous foot, but the bird cried out in a roar, "STOP! HERM!!" Herman ground to a slippery halt, and the wren landed on his toe. Herman picked up the tiny bird on his trunk, lifted him up to eye level, and exclaimed, "Willie! You got spectacles! I almost didn't recognize you! I could-da killed you!"

NCTE Standard for Language Arts: Students employ a wide range of strategies as they write and use different writing process elements appropriately to communicate with different audiences for a variety of purposes.

Producing a Storyboard

Illustration	Illustration	Illustration	Illustration	Illustration
Text	Text	Text	Text	Text

ASSIGNMENTS AND GUIDELINES:

This week, you will be working with a partner to design a storyboard. Storyboards are used by moviemakers, television producers, and advertising firms to show the most meaningful scenes of a story, commercial, or some other program. You will follow these guidelines as you work this week:

1. You will work with a partner to develop a story line either from those given at the right or one of your own.
2. After you have the story idea, take the main parts of your story as shown on the right and write these out on index cards, glue them to the board provided by your teacher, and illustrate the part above the text as shown.
3. Brightly color the illustrations. Share your work with the class.

As you may recall, one of the very basic themes of stories is: **Beautiful girl loves a boy who loves someone else. She is pursued by another boy but never loves him and casts him aside in hopes that she will finally win the love of her life. Finally, she is left all alone due to her selfish and egotistical behavior.**

STORY LINE SAMPLES:

1. One idea for a story is about a young boy named Peter who has a crush on the most beautiful girl in the class. This girl, Vicky, however, is a real creep of a person. She is unkind and heartless. Peter has another friend named Julia, and she is secretly in love with him. Julia tells him that the beautiful girl Vicky is no good, but he still pursues her. Finally, he loses Julia, and Vicky goes out with him once and tosses him aside. He is left all alone.
2. Another idea is about a girl named Trang. Trang is a beautiful girl, but she is thoughtful and shy. The first day of school in this country, she meets and falls for a boy named Paulo who notices that she is lost in the school and takes her to the correct class. Paulo is a basketball hero and does not even recall helping Trang. He is only concerned with sports and the glory it brings him. As the years pass, Trang finally gets over Paulo and finds a gentle boy named Hans and falls in love with him. At the same time, Paulo finally notices Trang, asks her out on a date, but she refuses him.

NCTE Standard for Language Arts: Students employ a wide range of strategies as they write and use different writing process elements appropriately to communicate with different audiences for a variety of purposes.

Rags to Riches

ASSIGNMENTS AND GUIDELINES:

This week, you will work with a partner to write a story summary based on the old theme "Rags to Riches." After you write the story, you will adapt it as a screenplay. After the teacher hears the summary of your story, he/she may permit you to further cast and direct the screenplay if time permits. Your assignments are as follows:

1. You will develop a story based on the basic "Rags to Riches" plot.
2. In the story, you must have a poor, forsaken character in a desperate situation. You may also have a villain, a hero, or a person who enables the poor character to become rich, plus any other characters.
3. The story that you write must be easily adapted into a play. In other words, you should have passionate characters moving from tragedy to happiness with great emotion.
4. You will write the story, revise and edit it completely, and hand it in to your teacher.
5. The teacher will pick two or three of the stories, and if yours is chosen, you will develop the story into a screenplay. In the screenplay, remember to list props, character movements, and suggested set designs.
6. You will choose persons to play in the screenplay, rehearse, and direct the play. Perform the play, and videotape it.

SUGGESTION FOR STORY:

Janie left home on a stormy autumn morning. She was ready for anything—well, just about anything. She was going to be a star; she felt it, even as the rain soaked through her threadbare coat, chilling her. The train to New York was late, and as she boarded it, her suitcase burst forth in the aisle, spilling its contents. She gathered her only belongings in a heap and found a seat. The hours passed, and her stomach ached with hunger, but she was determined to save every cent to help get her through the months ahead. When the New York skyline appeared through the mist, her heart skipped a beat. She rented a tiny room in a rundown boardinghouse and spent her first nickel on the "Play Bill," an ad listing jobs available on and off Broadway. She rose early each day and retired late each night. Thanksgiving came and went, and so did some of Janie's spirit. Three days before Christmas, on a dark, snowy night, she stepped from the doorway of her last audition, tired, worn-down, and hungry. Suddenly, her heel broke, and she collapsed on the curb, in tears. When she opened her eyes, she saw something lying in the gutter at her feet...

NCTE Standard for Language Arts: Students adjust their use of spoken, written, and visual language (e.g., conventions, style, vocabulary) to communicate effectively with a variety of audiences and for different purposes.

REGULAR GUY OR GIRL BECOMES A HERO!!

ASSIGNMENTS AND GUIDELINES:

This week, you will be working with a partner to do this assignment. You will each be writing a newspaper article about the other person. This character will have a heart of gold, and definite, <u>hidden</u> courage. Follow these guidelines as you write this week:

1. You will be pretending to be a school newspaper reporter.
2. You will write a newspaper article on a regular kind of student (your partner). This person suddenly had the opportunity to do something heroic. This part can be true or made-up. You will interview this character and he/she will tell you his/her exciting story. Then, your partner will interview YOU, and you will tell him/her about YOUR heroism (true or made-up). You will each develop your story into a thrilling article.
3. After you complete the story, either by hand or typing it on the computer, you will be cutting and pasting it to a larger piece of paper as shown on the right.
4. You will then illustrate this article either with a picture of the "hero," or with an illustration depicting the event.
5. You may wish to hang the "Front Page" articles all together on a bulletin board.

YOUNG GIRL SAVES KID BROTHER!

Shy little Shirley John from room 101, Mr. Carolina's homeroom, had the scare of her life last night, when she did a favor for her mom by watching her kid brother.

"It was about 9:00 p.m. and I had just tucked Billy (my kid brother) into bed. Billy is just three years old you see and, I have to admit, gets into a little mischief once in a while."

Shirley related this story to us last night, as police cars and fire engines lit up her street. "About 9:35, I had just switched to my favorite show, when I noticed a thin white cloud drifting slowly down the stairs in front of the TV screen. Then I smelled it! SMOKE! I ran up the stairs three at a time and found Billy in the bathtub crying and a fire raging at the foot of his bed in a pile of paper. I quickly threw the blanket over the fire, lifted Billy, and ran downstairs to call 911. Billy suddenly jumped out of my arms and ran back up the stairs, yelling, 'I forgot my Teddy!'"...

ILLUSTRATION

NCTE Standard for Language Arts: Students adjust their use of spoken, written, and visual language (e.g., conventions, style, vocabulary) to communicate effectively with a variety of audiences and for different purposes.

REVISING YOUR WRITING

A REVISED SAMPLE:

Below is an edited piece of writing that you might have done another time. Now it is time to revise it or pizzazz it up. Do the changes right on this sheet, preferably in a colored pen. Remember, the idea of revision is to make your not-so-interesting writing really interesting. When you complete the sheet, discuss the corrections you made with a partner, and then hand in the sheet to your teacher. A couple of revisions are made for you below.

long, long ago ↓ far, far ↓

Once upon a time, in a land far away, there was a big dragon who lived in a ~~tree house~~ [cave]. He was a very lonely dragon because everyone ran away from him. He thought they were afraid of him because they thought he would eat them up in a big, big, big gulp. The dragon decided he would show the people of the village that he was nice. One day at dawn, he he picked a big bunch of sunflowers then he went to each house and knocked at the door ever so gently. He placed a sunflower at the feet of the owner.

REVISING A SAMPLE:

This is a completed revision of the writing to the left.

Once upon a time, long, long ago and far, far away, there was a dragon who lived in a cave. He was a very lonely dragon because everyone ran away whenever he came near. They thought he would eat them up. Also, he was scary looking. The dragon decided he would show the people of the village that he was nice. One day at dawn, he went to each house and knocked at the door, but when he said hello, he set everyone's roofs on fire because he was the kind of dragon that breathed fire. So, he failed. As he slowly walked home to his cave, he was very sad. Suddenly a little bluebird landed on his shoulder and said, "Don't be sad. That was just your first try. Now you will have to think of some other way to meet the people. Let's put our heads together and think of what we can do to make the people like you. Remember the old saying, 'Try, try again.'" So, the next morning he went out and picked a huge bunch of sunflowers, went to each house, and then placed a flower on each doorstep. He knocked on the door and when the person answered the door, he gave them a big smile. They all slammed the door in his face, but a couple of children returned his smile. He was so very happy! He now had made some progress.

NOW, it is time for you to make your OWN story. Then edit and revise it, and edit it again. Then put it in final form and hand in all of the copies to your teacher.

NCTE Standard for Language Arts: Students use a variety of technological and information resources (e.g., libraries, databases, computer networks, videos, maps) to gather and synthesize information and to create and communicate knowledge.

ROBIN HOOD

ASSIGNMENTS AND GUIDELINES:

This week, you will be making a "Wanted" poster asking for the arrest of the famed Robin Hood of Sherwood Forest. You will work with a partner to complete the following assignments:

1. You will do research on the fictional character, Robin Hood.
2. You will take notes finding information about his life, how he came to be a thief, his loves, Sherwood Forest, the characters that accompany him, and his philosophy.
3. You must decide who is hunting him down and post a reward for his capture.
4. You will place all of this material together in an orderly way, trying to write in the "Old English" manner.
5. Place this information on a poster, with illustrations and anything else that will make it look like an authentic poster. Share the poster with the class.
6. Finally, choose an idea from the box on the right for extra credit, or as your teacher instructs.

IDEAS FOR A ROBIN HOOD STORY:

1. Write a story based on the story of Robin Hood, but this time, make him a modern-day person who robs from the rich to give to the poor.
2. Write a story of Robin Hood's young life that gives a logical reason for his development.
3. Write a story of Robin Hood after he retires from the life of a thief. What does he do? Where does he go?
4. Write a story with a totally different outcome from the actual tale. Perhaps Robin loses the Lady Marian to one of his friends, or perhaps the king never returns and Robin is caught and thrown in jail.
5. Write a story as if it were an autobiography of Robin Hood from his point of view.

NCTE Standard for Language Arts: Students participate as knowledgeable, reflective, creative, and critical members of a variety of literacy communities.

Romeo and Juliet

ASSIGNMENTS AND GUIDELINES:

This week, you will be developing a story that will be written alone or with a partner to tell about two persons who eyewitnessed the entire horrible story of Romeo and Juliet, and you will relate their stories. These personalities would know every single event that transpired between the two star-crossed lovers. They might be eavesdroppers, interfering mothers-in-law, or a landlady/meddler type. In other words, they know every detail of the event and are VERY eager to relate their story. The following is a list of your assignments for the week. You may work with a partner or alone. Follow your teacher's instructions.

1. You will write a story as told to a reporter or the police of the events that took place before the tragic deaths of Romeo and Juliet.
2. The story will be a monologue or a dialogue.
3. After you have completed the monologue or dialogue, revise and edit your script, write it in final form, and memorize the part(s).
4. Perform what you have done on the assigned day.

SAMPLE SELECTION:

As you know, I am merely the poor, humble priest who happened to marry these two youngsters. How was I to know it would end in such a tragic manner? I watched them carefully for the few weeks after they were united in marriage, and I have never, in my 30 years of ministering, seen two happier youngsters. I saw them the day they met at the Feast of All Saints. They saw each other for the first time while eating the sweet fried dough that the widow Shelby prepared. Juliet had sugar upon her lips, and Romeo stood next to her. As their eyes met, I knew that they would look no longer for love, for they had found it. Romeo said some words to her, I could barely hear, but I believe them to be:

"How is it, that the sun hath shown so warmly upon me this day? That I hath the fortune to look upon a face of such beauty?" Or something to that effect.

She then replied, "What glorious angels are watching over me, that I have had the same good fortune?"

At that, they walked away together, and the rest of the story of these young lovers developed thus...

NCTE Standard for Language Arts: Students participate as knowledgeable, reflective, creative, and critical members of a variety of literacy communities.

SCIENCE FICTION WEEK

ASSIGNMENTS AND GUIDELINES:

This week, we will be writing a science fiction story. You probably have spine-tingling ideas for a story, but there are a few suggestions to help you in the far right column. These are the assignments for the week:

1. Complete the first draft of your story.
2. Share your story with your literature group.
3. Your group will make kindly suggestions and comments.
4. Go back to your seat and make revisions using the suggestions you received.
5. Complete one final draft, which must be written without error.
6. Make a full-color cover for your final draft with the title of your story in bold letters and a full-color illustration on the front.
7. You may include other illustrations within the story.
8. Share your final story with your literature group once again. They will critique your work.

SUGGESTIONS FOR STORY LINES:

Here are some ideas for a story line, or certainly, you may use your own:

1. One night, you are sleeping and are suddenly awakened by a bright light in your backyard. You look out and see an enormous spaceship landing in your backyard. It is doing so without ANY noise at all! Suddenly, the door slides open and...
2. You have been off from school for summer vacation and have noticed that your mom has been <u>insisting</u> that you drink your pink grapefruit juice EVERY DAY, three times a day, for the past four days. Also, all your family is acting kind of weird. One night, your mom asks you to put your little brother to bed, and as you are pulling his pajama top over his head, you notice he has a metal arm band at the top of his arm...
3. One day in May, you come zooming home from school. You bound up the stairs to change clothes, go to your closet, pull the door open, and there...
4. The news made the announcement last week that the Earth has been invaded by Martians. Could it be true? Then one day there is a knock on your front door. What happens next is unbelievable...

NCTE Standard for Language Arts: Students employ a wide range of strategies as they write and use different writing process elements appropriately to communicate with different audiences for a variety of purposes.

ASSIGNMENTS AND GUIDELINES:

This week, you will be creating settings that PAINT a picture for the reader. You have read many selections that do this for you, but now you will use your own creativity and visual memory to reproduce images on paper. Some "setting starters" are given on the right. You may find them helpful, or you may want to "paint" an entirely different setting. Your assignments are as follows:

1. You are to develop four settings. A setting includes:
   a. What you can see around you, wherever you are.
   b. It also consists of the time in which your story takes place, whether it be the past, present, or future. It may include a time and place that has never existed or will never exist, except in writing or in someone's mind, as in *Alice in Wonderland.*
2. After you write the first draft of these settings, you are to revise and edit them and make a final draft.
3. On the poster you have been given, you are to illustrate all four of your settings.
4. On the final day, be prepared to share your writing and poster with the class.

SETTING STARTERS:

1. It was bitterly cold outside when I awoke. Snow covered the grass, trees, and barn. The cows were crying to get out, unaware of the bitter cold and that the grass, their morning meal, was covered by a blanket of glistening white...
2. We have just landed on Jupiter's Moon, Io, suspected of having life for the past century. The atmosphere appeared to be blood red, as seen from the portholes of the ship. We drew straws which decided that I would be the first to investigate the territory. I suited up and descended into the compression chamber. The door opened at my feet, and the ladder slid out of the bowels of the ship...
3. It was Halloween night, and we went out trick-or-treating. Teddy challenged me to go into the old Harrison place and go through every room once. He said if I could do it, he'd tell all the guys at school, and I would be a hero...
4. It was Thanksgiving Day, and I awoke later than usual. Mom called me down to fetch eggs from the henhouse. I slipped on my long johns and my overalls and proceeded down the back stairs into the warm kitchen. The fire was roaring in the fireplace as kettles steamed. Enticing smells of the dinner roasting in the oven filled the room...

NCTE Standard for Language Arts: Students employ a wide range of strategies as they write and use different writing process elements appropriately to communicate with different audiences for a variety of purposes.

TALL TALE CHARACTERS

ASSIGNMENTS AND GUIDELINES:

Tall tales have always been lots of fun, but it is the characters that make them so interesting. Tall tale characters can do just about anything! To refresh your memory, some characters are Paul Bunyan, Pecos Bill, John Henry, and Davy Crockett. They accomplished supernatural feats, such as lassoing a tornado, digging the Grand Canyon with an enormous blue ox called Babe, digging a tunnel faster than the most efficient machine in existence, and many others. Here is a list of your assignments:

1. First you will design a NEW tall tale character. To do this, it may be interesting to see if you can draw a picture of her or him and then tell about her/his personality. Write about the character's likes and dislikes. Describe what makes her/him able to perform phenomenal feats and the things she/he can do.
2. Outline a plot, and then write a story with your character or characters involved in solving some kind of problem and saving lots of people, children, or a city.
3. Finally, print your story on the long strips of paper provided by your teacher and make a cover for the story.
4. Be prepared to share a summary of your story with the class.

STORY IDEAS:

1. One day, long ago, there was an old woman who had a son. Very early in the son's life, the mother noticed that his teeth were exceptionally strong. He could crack black walnuts in his mouth and pick up bricks with his teeth when he was still just a lad. One stormy day, a mean, dark-looking man appeared at the door of their home and said that they had to move because a huge dam was being built that would flood the very land where their house stood...

2. There once lived a little girl who had long curls and sweet pink cheeks. But, she was anything but sweet. Not that she was sour, mind you, but she could kick a mule across the county and back! She had legs that had the strength of ten men...

NCTE Standard for Language Arts: Students use spoken, written, and visual language to accomplish their own purposes (e.g., for learning, enjoyment, persuasion, and the exchange of information).

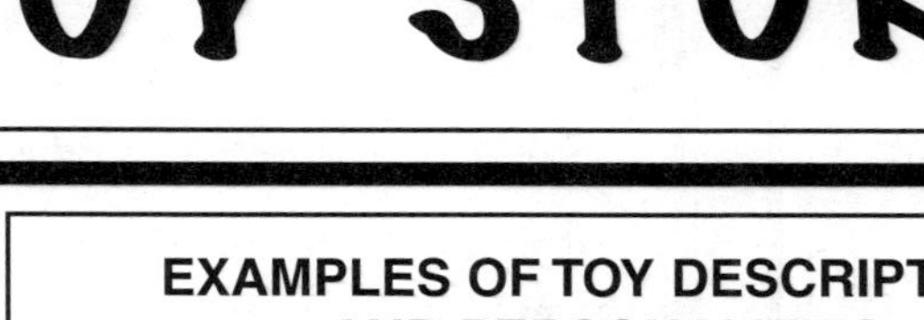

ASSIGNMENTS FOR THE WEEK:

This week, you will be writing a story about a toy that comes to life. The well-known story "Pinocchio" is a story of this type. The following is a list of your assignments for the week:

1. You are to write five good paragraphs, each paragraph describing one different toy personality, how it comes to life, the personality of the toy, and at least one adventure each toy might experience.
2. After your characters are designed, write a short outline listing the events of the story you will write this week. You will write a selection with one or more of the characters you have designed.
3. Write your story, edit, and revise. Then do the final draft.
4. Make a drawing or replica of your toy.
5. Make an illustrated cover for the story.

EXAMPLES OF TOY DESCRIPTIONS AND PERSONALITIES:

1. My first toy is a little metal truck I got for one of my early birthdays. This truck is special because it was made in Panama. My Aunt Alfreda got it for me on one of her world travels. Anyway, one day I was down in the damp, dark basement, separating recyclable materials, and I hear this rattling sound coming from this old battered box under the steps, then I heard, in a small voice ... "Señorita!"...

2. My second toy is my calculator in school. Talk about embarrassing! One day last week, we were having calculator races, and after a few minutes, my calculator started to show the words, "Hi," and "How are you, Mo?" (That's my name, Mo.) Well the calculator would NOT do the work I was punching in, so I decided to go to the restroom where I could bang it on something and bring it back to its senses. It was hopeless. When I got to the restroom, it printed out a message, in one or two words at a time. "It," said that <u>I</u> had been selected by another galaxy, to complete a task...

EXAMPLE OF AN OUTLINE:

1. I discover that my toy truck from Panama can speak Spanish.
2. My toy truck has been wakened by a "Force" that guards all toys and only wakens them to go on life-saving missions.
3. My truck has spoken to me because it needs me to help it in the job it has been sent to do.
4. Since I cannot speak Spanish, I enlist the help of a boy in my class named Enrico.
5. The first task we must do is stow away on a train bound for New Hampshire. We go to a small village named Dunleigh, in search of a boy named Carlos.
6. Carlos needs a bone-marrow transplant, and I find <u>I</u> have the matching blood type!
7. We contact my parents, they fly up, Carlos recovers, and I have a new friend, Enrico!!

NCTE Standard for Language Arts: Students use a variety of technological and information resources (e.g., libraries, databases, computer networks, videos, maps) to gather and synthesize information and to create and communicate knowledge.

TRUTH IN ADVERTISING

ASSIGNMENTS AND GUIDELINES:

This week, you will be analyzing television commercials. You will work in a cooperative group to gather information, and then you will bring the information together to decide what you want to use for the assignment and what is unnecessary. The following lists your assignments for the week:

1. You will watch one hour of daytime or evening television.
2. During this hour, you will record statements made about products during the commercials, which perhaps are exaggerated or untrue. Perhaps your family will help you gather the data. (On the right are statements to show you how to do this part of the activity.)
3. When your group has all the statements they gathered as a group, you will begin analyzing the truthfulness of each statement. You will categorize the statements you gather in the following ways:
   a. The statement is ABSOLUTELY TRUE AT ALL TIMES.
   b. The statement is TRUE PART OF THE TIME.
   c. The statement COULD BE TRUE.
   d. The statement is NEVER TRUE.
4. Finally, rewrite the commercial, making it truthful and pizzazzy. Share what you found with the class.
5. Place all your information on a poster as shown on the right.

ABSOLUTELY TRUE
1. Everyone needs to bathe or shower sometimes.
2. We all need to eat.
3. We all like some kinds of food.
4. We all need to be loved.

TRUE SOMETIMES
1. We love candy.
2. We all eat some kind of breakfast.
3. We all love jelly on our toast.
4. We have to have sugar.

COULD BE TRUE
1. Kids love cereal.
2. Pizza is our favorite dish.
3. Spaghetti is great for you.
4. Shower gel makes you feel smooth.
5. Kids love adventure.

NEVER TRUE
1. Soap kills all bacteria.
2. Everyone loves candy.
3. Apples make you healthy.
4. Food supplements are good for everyone.
5. A certain company makes all good things.

NCTE Standard for Language Arts: Students use spoken, written, and visual language to accomplish their own purposes (e.g., for learning, enjoyment, persuasion, and the exchange of information).

ASSIGNMENTS AND GUIDELINES:

This week, you will be working with a small group to develop characters and a plot for an "Ugly Duckling" story. Before you begin writing, it would be good idea to review the original "Ugly Duckling" story that was written by Hans Christian Andersen. Please follow the assignments listed below:

1. You are to develop a storyboard that tells the story of the characters of your story. This is the character who goes from ugly to beautiful in whatever manner you desire.
2. You will also write a brief summary of your story. A sample summary is located to the right.
3. Exchange your storyboard and summary with another group and have them discuss it with your group.
4. After you have done both assignments, prepare a class presentation about your "Ugly Ducking."

STORYBOARD

Megan at 10 coming to school	Charles at 10 walking down the hall	Megan at 20 in college	Charles at 20 in college	Megan and Charles meet

SUMMARY:

Our story tells of a girl, Megan, who lived in a small town. She was very thin with tons of freckles and crooked teeth. She had a crush on the most handsome boy at school, Charles Jamison, but he never even gave her a glance. She had no friends, and she was also very shy and lacked confidence. When she was 10, her family moved to another state. Amazingly, as she grew up, she became absolutely beautiful. She had her teeth straightened, and her freckles faded. When she went to college, she found, much to her delight, that Charles was going to the same school. One evening, she was invited to a party, and he was there also. He spotted her across the room and came to speak to her...

NCTE Standard for Language Arts: Students use spoken, written, and visual language to accomplish their own purposes (e.g., for learning, enjoyment, persuasion, and the exchange of information).

Writing a Telephone Conversation

ASSIGNMENTS AND GUIDELINES:

For this week's writing, you will follow the guidelines listed below:

1. This week, you will write a telephone script for two characters.
2. At the beginning of the script, give a brief description of each character and the time of day it is taking place. Also describe the places where each character is located at the time of the call.
3. This script can take place anywhere and at any time of the day.
4. Try to include some suspense in the script or a mystery that is slowly being uncovered. A sample script is given in the box on the right.
5. With a partner, practice reading the script. Then be prepared to read your script with your partner for the class.
6. If time permits, perhaps you can critique each other's characters and scripts. What did you like about the script or the characters, and what suggestions do you have?

SAMPLE SCRIPT:

This is a sample conversation that is taking place between a receptionist and an actor. One Saturday evening, they are speaking on the telephone for the first time.

TODD: *Hi, June. I got your name and phone number from the "Lonely Hearts Electronic Computerized Dating Guild." I just thought I'd give you a buzz and ask you if we could have dinner some night. Wad-da-ya-say?*

JUNE: *I never go out with strangers. Tell me about yourself.*

TODD: *Well, I was born in Buffalo, New York, during one of the biggest snowstorms in history. My mother called a cab because my dad was stuck in the snow somewhere. The cab came, and Mother didn't make it to the hospital. I was delivered by a tough six-foot-six cabdriver. When I was five, both Mother and Father died in one of the only plane crashes at the Buffalo Airport, and I went to live with my grandpa in Oregon. I went to the University of Nebraska on a football scholarship. I work for the Growler Fishery as a Production Manager, but I'm trying to break into acting. How about you?*

JUNE: *I can't stand fish. Well, I was born in Wabashah, Minnesota, and I was the youngest of six kids. After graduation, I waitressed in five cities in Oregon and despised every second of it. Now I work as a receptionist.*

NCTE Standard for Language Arts: Students employ a wide range of strategies as they write and use different writing process elements appropriately to communicate with different audiences for a variety of purposes.

WRITING DESCRIPTIONS

ASSIGNMENT 1

This week you will be writing several types of descriptive selections. To begin, you will choose one of the following persons to describe:

1. Your best friend
2. A good friend
3. Someone you would like to have as a friend
4. A close member of your family

After you have thought of a good person to describe, begin writing a DETAILED description of that person. Describe him or her from head to toe! Be very specific, telling exact colors that describe him or her. Use comparative words. Be sure to tell the following things:

1. What he or she looks like
2. What kind of tastes he or she has (in clothes, for instance)
3. His or her likes and dislikes
4. An experience you recall having with him or her

ASSIGNMENT 2

Today, you will write about OBJECTS. You will choose any object and describe it completely. In your description, you will not say WHAT it is that you are telling about. We will share these in our groups or with partners to see if they can guess what it is that we wrote about. Some of the objects you may want to choose from are:

1. A favorite toy
2. A game that you play
3. Your bedroom
4. A well-used room in your home
5. Our classroom
6. Your secret place
7. Your house

Whatever you choose to describe, start at one point and move away from that point as you continue to describe the object in writing. Check over your work completely, correcting your spelling and grammar errors. Then write a final draft.

ASSIGNMENT 3

Today, you will write about something that exists only in your imagination. Some things you could describe are:

1. A planet you visited in a dream
2. A space alien you imagined
3. A creature that appeared in your attic
4. A fairy tale hero
5. Yourself, as you become the new "Super Person"
6. A new, unheard-of animal
7. A castle in which you will live in the future
8. A city of the future

After you do a detailed description of this imaginary item, check it over and correct the spelling and grammar errors. Be prepared to write a final draft.

ASSIGNMENT 4

For the final assignment of the week, you will describe an ACTION. For instance, you may choose to describe the production of a peanut butter sandwich. There are many, many steps to this relatively simple act. You may choose from the following to write about or choose one of your own wonderful ideas. Whatever you do, please make sure that you know how to do this activity very well. Some examples are:

1. How you play a particular game, like basketball or soccer
2. How to clean your room
3. How to make a dinner salad with meat and cheese
4. How to do a science fair experiment
5. How to play a board game with which you are familiar
6. How to do an activity that not very many people know how to do, like ride a horse or plant a garden

After you write your directions, correct all your errors and do a final draft. Both are to be handed in to the teacher.

NCTE Standard for Language Arts: Students employ a wide range of strategies as they write and use different writing process elements appropriately to communicate with different audiences for a variety of purposes.

WRITING FABLES

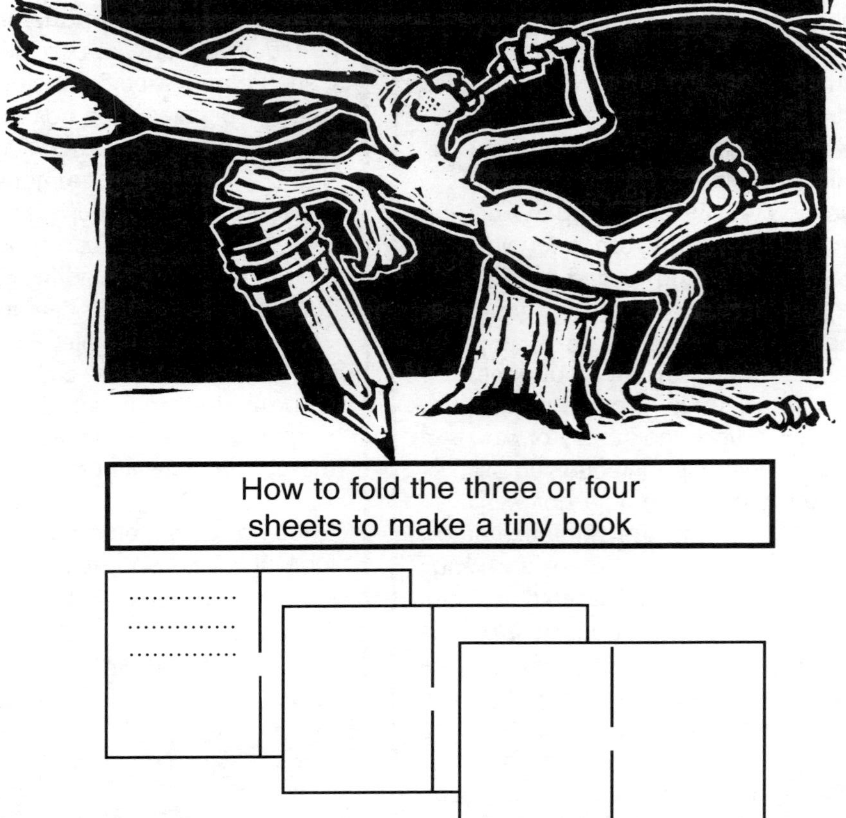

ASSIGNMENTS AND GUIDELINES:

This week, you will be working alone to write a fable, and then you will print it in a tiny book. A fable, as you recall, is a brief story that has a lesson within it and concludes with the moral of the story.

One fable of which you may have heard is the story "The Tortoise and the Hare." In this story, the hare challenges the tortoise to a race because the hare is proud and arrogant and believes that he could beat the tortoise even if he walked! As the story goes, the hare is SO confident that he lies down to take a nap halfway though the race! The tortoise never stops for a rest but keeps on plugging, slowly but surely. The moral of this story is, "Slow and steady wins the race." Keep this in mind as you write your own fable. These are your assignments for the week:

1. The first thing to do is think of the moral you would like to portray. Some morals are listed on the right for your use.
2. The next step is to develop an outline for your story. Be sure to stick to the idea you had for the moral of your story as you write the outline.
3. Next, write the first draft of your story. Revise and edit the draft, and then make your little book.
4. To make a small book, you will need three or four pieces of a heavier stock paper cut into pieces 10″ wide by 6″ high. Fold the papers in half as shown to the right.
5. Draw lines, with a pencil and ruler, on each side of the booklet where you will print. Reserve the front side for the cover of your tiny book. Illustrate where you think it is necessary.

How to fold the three or four sheets to make a tiny book

EXAMPLES OF MORALS TO USE:

1. Better late than never.
2. It is easy to despise what you cannot get.
3. The value of money is not measured by how much money you have, but how it is spent.
4. We often condemn those for what we ourselves practice.
5. One good turn deserves another.
6. United we stand, divided we fall.
7. Those who have the most, complain the most.
8. No matter how long it takes, people get what they deserve.
9. You can't tell a book by its cover.

NCTE Standard for Language Arts: Students employ a wide range of strategies as they write and use different writing process elements appropriately to communicate with different audiences for a variety of purposes.

WRITING FROM ANOTHER POINT OF VIEW

ASSIGNMENTS AND GUIDELINES:

This week, you will be writing a common story or fairy tale told by another character in that story. For instance, we always hear the story of Cinderella as if Cinderella is the poor, tortured sister, but what if you interviewed one of the stepsisters? What do you think the stepsister would have to say? What about a story from the fairy godmother's point of view? How about "Sleeping Beauty" as told by the wicked witch?

Your assignment this week is to write **three** short stories from another point of view. Here are your guidelines:

1. You will think of three common stories you have heard since you were a kid. Then you will think of another character in that story and begin writing the story from that character's viewpoint.
2. You will write three first drafts, edit and revise these as completely as you can, and then choose your best one.
3. You will write **one** final draft that is without error.
4. You will then memorize the story (if possible) and prepare a presentation for the class, speaking as if you really ARE that person.

COMMON STORY TITLES

1. Cinderella
2. Pinocchio
3. The Three Little Pigs
4. The Steadfast Tin Soldier
5. Aladdin and His Wonderful Lamp
6. Oliver Twist
7. Jack and the Beanstalk
8. The Ugly Duckling
9. Beauty and the Beast
10. Little Red Riding Hood
11. David Copperfield

(There are many more stories from which you may choose, as long as they are familiar.)

EXAMPLES TO HELP YOU:

This is written from the wicked stepsister's point of view in Cinderella:

The day we moved into that house, let me tell you, was the day my life became a rotten mess! That little wishy-washy Cinderella was a two-faced, lying, little manipulator! She got me in more hot water with my mother than you'll ever know. And all that junk you've heard about her winning the heart of the prince with her beauty, well that's a lot of BUNK! Here's the REAL low-down...

This is written from the point of view of the cow in "Jack and the Beanstalk."

I was just a regular kind of good old cow producing milk just like Jack and his mother wanted, when out of the blue one day, Jack's mother tells him he has to go out and sell me to get some money because they needed food too, not just milk. Imagine my surprise when Jack tied a rope around my neck. He was crying while he did so, because Jack and I were the best of friends. However, Jack was not the sharpest tack in the box, and along the way, he met a man who told Jack that he had five MAGIC beans, and if he planted them, they would grow overnight!...

NCTE Standard for Language Arts: Students use spoken, written, and visual language to accomplish their own purposes (e.g., for learning, enjoyment, persuasion, and the exchange of information).

Writing Fun With Idioms

ASSIGNMENT GUIDELINES:

Idioms are so much a part of our language, we probably are unaware that we are using them. To become more aware of these oddities of our language, we will write a story this week using some of these in the LITERAL sense. That means, when we use the idiom "hurry up," we will use it to mean hurry UP as in, hurry up "into the clouds" or hurry up "from the basement." With a partner, write a story that will probably sometimes sound silly, and then share these in class or with a small group.

SOME IDIOMS:

1. **dancing on a cloud**
2. **runs like a deer**
3. **raining cats and dogs**
4. **fast as lightning**
5. **born in a barn**
6. **eats like a horse**
7. **pretty as a picture**
8. **swims like a fish**
9. **hard as a rock**
10. **eat your words**
11. **lies like a rug**
12. **can't hit the broad side of a barn**
13. **smart as a whip**
14. **bite the bullet**
15. **pain in the neck**
16. **dead as a doornail**
17. **let the cat out of the bag**
18. **dark as pitch**
19. **bells on her toes**
20. **pure as the driven snow**
21. **barking up the wrong tree**
22. **don't beat around the bush**
23. **don't blow your top**
24. **burning the midnight oil**

SAMPLE SILLY STORY USING IDIOMS:

When I was born, my mama did look at me, and then she says to Pa, "Well, Pa, he may not be playin' with a full deck, but he is as cute as a button."

Pa just grunted as he picked me up and said, "Yep and as pure as the driven snow."

Ma answered, "Look, Pa, he's hungry again, go out to the barn and get another bucket of oats. That boy sure in heck does eat like a horse. Why, he's gone through eight bowls of oats since this morning!"

"He might eat a lot, but he sure is as pretty as a picture, isn't he, Ma?"

NCTE Language Arts Standard: Students use spoken, written, and visual language to accomplish their own purposes (e.g., for learning, enjoyment, persuasion, and the exchange of information).

Writing Scary Stories

ASSIGNMENTS AND GUIDELINES:

This week, we will write a scary story. When you have finished all your work, you will hand in the following items:

1. Two character webs (a sample web is shown to the right)
2. One flow chart showing events of the story (also shown at the right)
3. One rough draft, which is edited and revised
4. One final draft, with or without a cover, typed or neatly written

Possible Titles:

1. The Cemetery
2. The Thing Under My Bed
3. My Worst Nightmare
4. The Night of the Witch
5. The Ghost in my Closet
6. The Haunted Attic
7. The Curse

Possible Story Starters:

1. I walked up the creaking stairs in the dead of night and heard a whisper come out of the darkness...
2. I opened my bedroom closet and there it was...
3. It was very quiet in my bedroom as I snuggled under the covers, and then I heard a tiny sound...
4. When my friend asked me to spend the night in the old Hamilton Place, I hesitated, because...
5. It was a chilling cold night, and I was home alone. There was a knock at the door, and when I pulled the door slowly open...
6. I walked up the creaking stairs leading to the attic. Cobwebs brushed across my skin. I got to the trapdoor and pushed it with my shoulder. When it opened, my heart came to a stop, for standing there in front of me was...

FLOW CHART:

Wilda was an ugly old witch who lived in the chimney of the old Swanson Place. The house was old and run-down. One day, a huge moving truck pulled up with furniture.

↓

The Toppolo family moved in, and Wilda was so mad, she was steaming from both ears. She decided to "scare" them out of the house by planning nightly freaky events.

↓

1st night, she dragged chains across the attic floor all night. The 2nd, she rolled acorns across the bedroom floors of the parents and the boy. The 3rd, she rearranged all the furniture on the first floor of the house...

↓

By the eighth night, the Toppolo family stayed up all night, one person on each floor. They had bowls of candy and vases of flowers to offer the "evil spirit" as a sign of peace. Wilda was so upset by these actions that she ran away and never came back!

CHARACTER WEB:

(NAME OF CHARACTER) **Wilda**

- She is uglier than a troll. She has orange skin and a long green nose.
- She lives in a chimney of the old Swanson place, now occupied by the Toppolo family.
- She is very angry that they live in HER house. She decides to get rid of them.
- Every night she tries something scary to get them out.

NCTE Standard for Language Arts: Students use spoken, written, and visual language to accomplish their own purposes (e.g., for learning, enjoyment, persuasion, and the exchange of information).

Writing Song Lyrics

ASSIGNMENTS AND GUIDELINES:

This week, you will be working with a partner to rewrite words to three songs that you already know. The following are the lists for your assignments:

1. You will write the words to three tunes that you know.
2. One tune has to be a childhood song that you learned, perhaps as a jump rope song or a singing round when you were young.
3. Another tune has to be a common older song, Broadway song, or patriotic song—a song that "everyone" knows.
4. The final song may be any modern song. Remember to choose the song and write your words carefully, so you could perform it for younger children or tape it for the morning news show.
5. Finally, print your lyrics on chart paper for a sing-along. You do not have to perform your songs, but the class can sing them as long as they have the words. Be prepared to share the words to the songs with the class, or perform them, or both.

SAMPLE LYRICS TO "ROW, ROW, ROW YOUR BOAT":

Swim, swim, swim to Mars,
through the atmosphere,
butterfly, butterfly, butterfly stroke,
grin from ear to ear!...

LYRICS TO "I'VE BEEN WORKING ON THE RAILROAD":

I've been doing all my homework every single night,
I've been doing all my homework, just to make my parents glad,
Don't you think that I'm the greatest,
And not only smart, I will be another genius,
When I do grow up...

LYRICS TO "TAKE ME OUT TO THE BALLGAME":

Did you open the toothpaste?
Did you squeeze it all out?
Over the toilet and on the tub?
Are you some kind of little nut?...

LYRICS TO "OLD McDONALD HAD A FARM":

Old Piano had a flaw, oh, oh, oh, oh, oh
we called a person who fixed it up, oh, oh, oh, oh, oh
With a tap, tap here and a bang, bang there...

LYRICS TO "FRERE JACQUES":

Easter bunnies, little chickies, colored eggs, colored eggs,
Anyway you want them, anyway you want them,
red or blue, red or blue...

LYRICS TO "JINGLE BELLS":

Happy snails, happy snails sliding cross the lane
Oh what fun they have in grass ... everytime they eat ... eat...
Happy snails, happy snails, over the flowers, they are slow and
happy snails ... no matter what they do...